It's About HIM

Where Listening Leads

SHERRY L. SCHOENING

ISBN 978-1-64299-487-2 (paperback)
ISBN 978-1-64299-489-6 (hardcover)
ISBN 978-1-64299-488-9 (digital)

Copyright © 2018 by Sherry L. Schoening

All rights reserved. No part of this publication may be reproduced, distributed, or transmitted in any form or by any means, including photocopying, recording, or other electronic or mechanical methods without the prior written permission of the publisher. For permission requests, solicit the publisher via the address below.

Christian Faith Publishing, Inc.
832 Park Avenue
Meadville, PA 16335
www.christianfaithpublishing.com

Printed in the United States of America

Chapter One

The Beginning

Well, you know how valuable feedback can be, when I just told my fourteen-year-old daughter that I wanted to write a book, she gave me that look, you know the one, the you-are-outside-your-mind look, that look that only teenagers can give effectively without saying a word. Well, in spite of her encouragement, I am going to hit the keys. I tried the pen, too many mistakes, then the pencil, but my eraser was worn to the metal before the first page was done. I decided if I wrote it and then typed it, this project will take me twenty years, and well, I don't have twenty years to spend on this project. I am anxious and excited to put down on paper or onto the screen, as it is for many tablet fans, some of what my children consider normal life; others, however, have noted it as nontypical, it just sounds better than abnormal, and they have encouraged me to document my "adventures."

Adventures, you say; yes, adventures. Why should a fifty-something wife, physical therapist, and mother of six not have adventures? You say growing up in a town of less than thirteen thousand does not sound like the setting for adventures. What if I told you I am from the Midwest, is that any more enticing? No? Well, you guys are a hard sell!

You are right, I am just an ordinary woman, living life, raising and loving my family, loving my friends, investing in my community and my church, and working to bless those patients which come through the doors of our clinic. Ordinary, that is me. I bet if you could find a current dictionary, you just might find my picture. Well, probably not, I hate pictures of myself. I am so ordinary that there are some people I have met three or four times, and each time I am introduced, it is like the first time meeting me, for them. Remembering me is not important. To be completely truthful, this story is not about ordinary me, it is much more about the extraordinary God I love and serve. Since my life is intertwined with Jesus, you have to understand who I am a bit to understand how God has shown up and revealed His reality, His faithfulness, His mercy, His grace, and His love.

Well, everyone knows you start a story at the beginning. Let's rewind a little more than fifty years ago. I was born into the typical American family; a mom and a dad who fell in love and got married. They met and married within a couple of months, which by today's standards would be considered reckless and downright crazy, but it was a different time.

My mother was raised in Nova Scotia as one of nine children. Her family moved to the States with part of her family due to the severe asthma my aunt suffered from; it had threatened to take my aunt's life several times. The doctors had told my grandparents that my aunt's best chance for survival was to move to a drier climate, such as Colorado or Arizona. They decided to settle in Colorado.

My mother had quit school and gone to work at fifteen. Her sisters all married around eighteen, so her family had almost given up hope that she would ever marry. Why, she was twenty-three years old and had been on her own working eight years already and had not found Mr. Right. As I said, it was a different time. She was wise and had no desire to just settle, so even though she had dated several potential suitors over the years, if she did not see any future with them, she cut them loose. She didn't see any sense in dating just to date; therefore, when she met my dad, she also didn't see any sense is dragging out the inevitable either; so when he proposed, it didn't make sense to wait.

IT'S ABOUT HIM

When my mother and father met, he was ending his time in the service and was stationed at Fort Carson, near the springs—Colorado Springs, that is. Well, not to drag this background on too long, they met, married, and started a family with yours truly first and my brother about eighteen months later. There were struggles getting started, and after about five years of marriage, Dad decided to bring his bride and family back to where he grew up, in Wabash, Indiana, for a new start.

I am proud to claim my Colorado birth, but I was only three when we moved, and most of my memories of Colorado fall back to our visits there. When we moved to Wabash, my parents rented a section of a large Victorian home, which contained the office of the optometrist who owned it. Even though we lived there only a year or so, I have many memories in that house. There were a few other apartments in it, and there were several characters who resided there. One such character was the adult son of a couple that occupied another apartment. Even though I was very young, I sensed that he was a little slow; why, he always tried to convince me that green was orange and that red was green. He also liked to pretend he took my nose and he was holding it. I decided to humor him, even though his thumb just didn't really pass as my nose.

There were other memories there, too. One of my earliest memories was coming into my parents' bedroom at night and finding my mom on her knees at the side of her bed. Like most three-year-olds, I had lots of questions, and I would ask, "Whatcha doin'?" She, being the loving, gentle, and patient woman she was, would stop, smile, and respond, "You're too young to understand, honey." Well, I might as well be transparent here, I was born with this stubborn streak. It is still with me, as a matter of fact, but I have had to do some taming with wisdom to minimize the trouble I get myself into. Of course, I was not satisfied with that answer, and I do not recall exactly how many times I asked and got the same answer, but I do know that eventually, I wore her down. Finally, one night, standing at the foot of her bed, with her on her knees, I asked the question again, and I finally got an answer, not just any answer, but the answer, which changed my life and prompted what has been my heart's cry my

THE BEGINNING

whole life. She said, "Honey, I am praying. I am praying to God, the creator of the universe and to His son Jesus, who died for my sins." Even at three, my spirit knew truth, and that statement caused something from deep within me to cry out, "I have to know Him!" That was the beginning, the beginning of my story, my life and my adventure.

Knowing our spiritual beginning is very important, and for many years, when people would talk about this pivotal date or moment that they accepted Jesus Christ as their savior, I could not remember the beginning of this journey, Jesus had just always been there for me. There were times that I remember thinking there was something wrong with me, that I could not pull out a date of this transformation from a life of sin to forgiveness. For a long time, I did not really believe I had a testimony to share, because God did not rescue me from drugs, alcohol, or a life of promiscuity. As I grew and matured though, I realized part of my testimony was that He spared me from those things. Even at three, I was in need of a Savior, and I already realized it. Background is important, that is why Genesis starts in the beginning. Most books of the Bible also contain these long lists of genealogy. It is important to know our past to understand where we are and who we are, and I know that God fills in the gap for those who don't know their beginnings, God being the loving father He is, grafts them right in. He grafted me in too, that was the work completed by Christ (Romans 11:23).

At the age of four, we moved into our own home, the one I would grow up in. It was in a quiet little neighborhood. My home was nestled between a few churches, one diagonal behind, one diagonal in front, and one on the corner behind my block. The block contained several families with young children and with several widows. It was the age in which mothers would sit and have coffee and visit each other's homes, where everyone knew each other and looked out for each other. We would typically stay on our block but ran free there. While the other kids played together, I would often go off to visit my friends, the widows. I guess you could say I was and am an old soul. You know, the serious one, one who wanted to get to the important stuff like how people were, really were, conversations about faith and stories about life and how things used to be. It is not to say I didn't enjoy humor and silliness, but my favorite times were engaging in conversations with adults, reading, and visiting the widows.

One of my favorite friends was Gertrude; she was one of the widows I visited. She had lost her husband when she was thirty-nine, and they never had any children. She was small and frail, with a hunched-over back, she wore a wig most of the time, and her house was like stepping back in time; she had inherited her grandmother's furniture and antiques, with a crystal chandelier and dark red velvet curtains. Her main sitting room contained an organ and a buffet which held her open Bible on top of it.

She would invite me in, and we would sit and sing while she played the organ, I believe it was with all three of us off key. We would sing hymns and make a joyful noise together. She would share stories of her growing-up years in Chicago. She shared about losing her mom at the age of three and being raised by her grandmother because her father didn't feel he could raise two daughters alone. My favorite stories were those that she shared about her faith. I remembered when she spoke of having read her Bible all the way through, I was amazed, looking at all those pages filled with so many words. It was hard to imagine anyone could read such a thick book; of course, most of my books at that time would have probably averaged a dozen words per page, making the prospect even more daunting.

Besides being stubborn, I also loved a challenge, so I decided that I would read the Bible all the way through. Next to deciding that I wanted to know God, reading my Bible at such a young age gave me an insight "well beyond my years," I was often told by adults. The impact that has had on my life, I may never fully realize. By the time I was eleven, I had completed the challenge, and what I learned was invaluable.

It was due to this knowledge that I was able to identify when things did not line up with God's Word. I fear that part of the struggle and battle in and for our culture stems from our not knowing what God's heart is and what His Word says, that makes it so easy for us to be tossed to and fro like on the waves (Ephesians 4:14).

THE BEGINNING

The church I grew up in had many godly people I loved, but I remember crying many times on my way home from church, disturbed at what I heard in both Sunday school and from the pulpit. My Sunday school teacher was a good man who taught his opinion and did not ever reference the Bible to back it up. I understood that without a real curriculum, it is easy to fall into that habit. The pastor was one who, I am sure, meant well, but would say things to stroke egos and prevent offending people; the result was watered down half-truths that ate at the core of me. I was worried about what eternity held for the people who did not know the importance of investing in reading their Bible to have that absolute standard to measure things by.

When I was eleven, the parsonage next to my home was invaded by a young new family: Dave, Deb, and Michael. It seemed that the house came to life when they moved in. They were very different than the previous occupants in many ways; for one thing, they almost immediately started connecting with the neighborhood. The previous pastor was an older man, and it was just him and his wife. I had seen them a few times but had never gotten to know them. There was a vibrancy in this young pastor and his wife, and I soon found that I could engage them in conversations about faith, and they encouraged me. It was so exciting to have this new resource. They were very patient and never made me feel like I was a bother.

This was also the age I was going through confirmation classes at my church. I struggled with this concept of coming of age, and if you completed the two years of classes, you were in. I was not sure what that meant exactly, but I understood it was meant to be significant.

During this timeframe, we tried to start a youth group at my church and failed. The church next door had an active youth group, and the pastor's wife suggested I might enjoy coming to their gatherings since I did not have that option at my church. It was wonderful to be in a large group of young people who enjoyed each other and learning about how to live this adventure of being a Christian.

When I completed my confirmation classes and was officially "confirmed," my spirit was disturbed. It was during our confirmation ceremony in front of the church, the pastor said, "This is the completion of what was started when you were baptized as an infant, you will now partake in Holy Communion and are a Christian with the rights of such, you will spend eternity in heaven." Now those may not have been his exact words, but they are close, and what I heard was this lie. I was shocked. These other preteens I was standing next to in robes were just told that this was their ticket to heaven. Nothing about truly understanding who Christ really was, what He did for us, or that free will and choice had anything to do with it. I was horrified, truly. I was friends with these kids and a couple kind of got it, but a couple were not ever really engaged in the classes or in things of faith. All I could think about was, "What if they believe this? Your parents signed you up, you are now a card-carrying member of the elite Christian club." That is when I checked out from that church. I could not be a part of this anymore. We did get a new pastor, and he really tried. At that point, however, it was about the doctrine and processes, not just the pastor and what was preached.

Bless my mom's heart, she loved it there, and she was fully invested and involved. I did not make it easy on her when I told her that I did not want to go there anymore. At first, she was reluctant, but since I could easily walk to the church next door and she did not want to hinder my growth, I started going there more.

I realize many churches are built on the structure and model of transitioning youth to membership and to communion with a similar process, and that is fine as long as they understand that you cannot make the decision for someone else, and not everyone truly comprehends it at the same time. It seems we would be doing a service to have one-on-one conversations about where they are in their journey and not set a "magic" age that you are supposed to understand. Faith in Christ cannot be scripted that way. It has to be about the relationship, not the traditions or religion for the sake of religion. Tradition does not replace a repentant heart and the personal commitment to follow Jesus and to live a life surrendered to Christ.

Chapter Two

Friends and Future

When it came to friends, I was so blessed. There are friends who I went all the way through school with who made commitments to Christ at a young age also, like my dear friend Lori. We were able to encourage each other and hold each other accountable. In fifth grade, Cheryl showed up and brought a new level of humor to my life. There was one girl who came into my life a little later and who became a part of my core group of friends. We were unlikely friends, her name was Cindy. She had gone to Catholic school but lived in Lori and Cheryl's neighborhood.

The way our community was set up, we had seven elementary schools funnel into our junior high, so in seventh grade, we met many new people. Cindy was one of the new people I met. She was an unlikely friend not because I had anything against her, rather she had something against me. She had told her mom she couldn't stand me because I was a "goody two-shoes." The amazing thing is, I didn't change, but something changed in her. She came to know Jesus, and all of a sudden, she saw me with a new light. Cindy was not just a friend; she and I became best friends, who shared many adventures together.

By the time we were in high school, my core group of friends each had their own circle of friends and spheres of influence. It was neat how this core group was the circle intersecting several others. It allowed us to develop more friendships and friends. I believe that is how the body of Christ is supposed to work.

We need to have a core group to encourage us, but that should not be our entire circle. God designed us for relationship, but he also commanded we reach a lost world. It may seem safe within the walls of your closest friendships, your home, or your church, but we were made for more than that. We were made to use the gifts and talents God has given all of His followers to reach those who do not know him. We need to make sure we are not keeping the Good News trapped behind doors and walls.

Late elementary and junior high was a formative time, more than I realized. It was during this time period I saw God working, directing, and molding me. What career I was interested in was one of the "things" I pondered during those years, and the adults around me would make suggestions. After being told by several people that my ability to state my case and stand my ground would help make me a great lawyer. I investigated this option. Law, justice—those ideals sounded noble. It was built in me to want to see justice and protect the underdog or misunderstood. When I thought about law, I would think of the judges in the Bible, like Solomon; somehow, I felt if I went that direction I would eventually want to be—a judge. It all sounded very interesting until someone explained our judicial process and how, as a lawyer, you are bound to be loyal to your client and to protect them from punishment. It ran through my thoughts, "You mean the goal is not to get to the truth? If my client is guilty, I have to work to get him off, even though I know of his guilt?" I could not reconcile myself with that, it did not seem like true justice to me, so no lawyering for me. Now, as an adult, I believe this is a career where Christians can make a huge impact to help bring justice and protect the people without a voice. It was not my calling, however.

When I was in middle school, we were instructed to do a report on a career we might be interested in. The reference book was huge, and I remember thumbing through the pages; and then I saw it, this picture of a lady teaching a little girl with leg braces how to walk. It reminded me of my resolve when my heart said, "I have to know

Him." That was the feeling I got when I saw the picture. That was my calling, I was certain.

It was not long after that I went to the guidance counselors in junior high and asked what classes I needed to take to help me be a physical therapist. It was that familiar look, "What planet are you from?" I gathered, from their expressions, that middle-school counselors did not get asked that very often by seventh and eighth graders. The research I had done told me I needed to be intentional, my odds of getting into PT school would be as or more difficult than medical school. Checking into the type of courses in PT school, I decided to focus on the sciences.

My research also revealed that you could have a 4.0 or equivalent, and if you did not have exposure or experience in a physical-therapy clinic, you were sunk. Being the large metropolis that my hometown was, there was one option to get the needed experience, the hospital physical therapy department. There were some high school students who worked in the department, so I decided I should get my name in the hat. An appointment was scheduled to go and speak to the director about potential jobs or shadowing.

He was a nice-enough guy, but he took one look at me and said he did not, nor would he ever have a job as an aide for me. He informed me it was nothing personal, but I was the wrong gender and did not have the required build. He stated he would love to help, but he only hired high school football players; his primary requirement was muscle. His theory was that he would last longer as a therapist if he had young strapping boys to do the heavy work. It made sense, but was very disheartening.

There was one way, he told me. His budget was limited, but the local vocational school had a health-occupations class, which he would be willing to take free help from. He assured me he would accept me if I went that route. Well, my options were limited, so that is exactly what I did. It was great experience, and the director appreciated my work ethic and interest. If we had any downtime, I would be studying his college and reference texts. My hunger for more knowledge was insatiable. He actually became my mentor. He encouraged me to apply at what was the second best PT school in the nation, and it was one of the few programs going to a master's degree, which he had informed me would be mandatory by 1990, just four to five years after I would be done. He suggested it made more sense to have the higher-level degree and experience. This seemed wise to me, and I applied and was accepted into undergraduate school at the same school I hoped to do my graduate work.

There were a couple more defining "adventures," which occurred before I finished high school. One of my dear friends was expressing his sadness that after numerous years of their home being TPed in the fall (when toilet paper is thrown into the trees and yard as a prank), this time-honored tradition was coming to an end as he was the youngest in his family, and because he was not that kind of cool, their home would no longer receive its annual fall decorating.

So, what does a good friend do when they hear something so sad? You make plans to TP his house. It was my TPing debut. Just as he was not that kind of cool, neither was I. With two friends in tow, I drove my father's Audi on this adventure. To add to the challenge, the house was down a long gravel driveway with a pond on one side and a steep ravine on the other.

Not having much experience at these things, I decided I should back in and stay at the front of the driveway near the road so I could make a quick getaway, because one thing I knew was that it was not cool to get caught; and even though I knew, this was a mercy TPing. I was sure his parents would not understand that. The car I was driving was a stick shift, and I put it in neutral and pulled up on the emergency brake. I opened the door, got out, and bent down to see beneath the trees to see if there were any house lights on.

Well, I don't know if there were any lights on or not, because I suddenly realized that the car was rolling. I must not have gotten the last click on the emergency brake and there was a downhill grade to the driveway. The way I had turned to look up at the house had me in a bad position to get back in easily, but I tried to turn and jump in, but before I knew what was happening, I was down and being dragged along the gravel driveway by my hand.

The car came to a halt, and the girls in the car were screaming like little girls; I knew what that phrase meant after that. When I got my bearings, I realized I was hanging by my right hand in the ravine. It was steep, but my back was supported by rocks. I looked around and saw that the driver's side back wheel was being held up by a five-inch branch on a tree, the front driver's side wheel was not on the ground at all, and I could not see if the passenger back tire was on the ground or not. I just prayed for wisdom and protection. (Boy, I should have prayed that before I got myself into this predicament.)

I tried to calm the girls and let them know I was alright, but someone had to get help. Neither wanted to move, but one finally cautiously got out and ran to the house. It was not long before my friend's dad had his tractor out trying to anchor the car so it did not roll on top of me. As I lay there, I just kept talking to God. I knew that there was something seriously wrong with my hand; I could not feel it at all, and I could tell that I was hanging by it. I reminded Him of my calling and asked Him how I was going to be able to do my job with one hand. Then a calm came over me, and I surrendered it to Him.

Even though we were out in the country, it did not take too long before I heard sirens. The ambulance was on the way. I was relieved until I heard the voices as the EMTs got out of the ambulance; it was my dad and another close friend, Pat. Great, I thought, "You try to do a kindness for a friend and look what happens." I don't think this could have gotten much more complicated.

They talked and problem solved a bit, then they did something with the door that freed my hand. Pat climbed down and carried me out. When we got up top, I looked down at my hand and it was a bloody mess, it was obvious there were several fractures and dislocations as I had zigzags from the top to bottom and from the sides. It was mangled. It was then I noticed I was having trouble standing on my foot; I must have hit a rock or sprained it on my joy ride.

They put me on the gurney, and Pat looked at my dad, and Pat was shaking more than me. He then had a one-sided conversation with my dad. He told him that this was like having one of his own kids hurt, and yes, he knew that I was his kid, but he handled these things better than him, so my dad was going to have to drive and he would sit with me in the back of the ambulance. The funny thing is, I don't remember Dad saying anything, he just got back in the ambulance to drive me to the hospital. Pat put a sheet over me to help take off the chill. As we bounced along that bumpy country road, he apologized but said he could not stand to look at my hand anymore and could he please cover it up, and he did. I assured him I understood, it was not much fun for me to look at either. When we got to the hospital, they took me by gurney to radiology and it was then they uncovered my hand. There was blood still on my hand but all the bones were back in place. They took an x-ray, and sure enough, no fractures. We just looked at each other with disbelief. God had healed my hand, miraculously healed it! The only remnant I had was a cut, now a scar on my index finger as a reminder of what God did. It was a few days later I found a poster of a rainbow with the phrase "Expect a Miracle." From that moment on, the rainbow was a reminder of God's faithfulness, guidance, and provision.

In the summer of my junior year, my best friend Cindy and I had the privilege to go on a short-term mission trip to Jamaica. We were on a team from several different states. Our assignment was to teach a vacation Bible school program in the mountains. We specifically were given the task of presenting Bible stories and the gospel through a puppet ministry. We had to practice with Jamie and Buster to make sure we moved their mouths at the same time ours moved. There is a little skill to that.

When we arrived in Jamaica, I was surprised by the need. As soon as we stepped out of the airport, we were surrounded by people with hands out asking for "a dolla," it was almost a chant. It was my first time experiencing firsthand what it felt like to be a minority. Our small group was made up of very pale people and we were in a mob of all very dark-skinned people. It was actually a little frightening to stand out so much. It was not like you could blend in.

I thought back to my hometown, where my school had two families of color, the Cosbys and the Jeffersons (no, I did not make up the names). Maybe because they grew up standing out, it didn't seem strange, but I suspected it was a challenge at times. Understanding how others feel is a blessing; it helps us relate in a different way.

FRIENDS AND FUTURE

As we drove through Kingston, I saw poverty I had never experienced before. Dwellings, you could not really call them houses, made from scrap pieces of metal, wood, and cardboard cluttered the landscape. There was a heaviness and a sadness I had never felt before, that people had to live like this, it broke my heart. This was the start of God showing me His heart, His compassion for all people.

When we arrived to our destination, we had been rattled around a bit by the unpaved road, the steep incline, and sharp turns. Our destination was the village in the mountains called Highgate. In this village were two orphanages, a girls and boys.

Our first stop was the boys' orphanage, and the sight is still one etched in my mind. The scene was beautiful with the flowering trees and foliage, with the contrast of a dozen little boys with machetes cutting the grass around the orphanage and a few playing with their pet goat. It was not long before I noticed that near the front door sat a little blue pickup and now there were a couple of men trying to get the goat into the bed of the truck, one pushing and one pulling. It was not just the site but the feeling. A calm and tranquility I had never experienced before came over me, I felt at home like I had never felt before. I loved this place and these people. Again, God was allowing me to sense His heart. I was where I was supposed to be, and I could have stayed there and not moved; I did not want the feeling to end. I believe that may have been the closest feeling to heaven I have ever known. Of course, the option to stay in that moment was short-lived. We dropped off the young men on the trip, and we were headed to the girls' orphanage where we would be staying.

There were girls of all ages at the girls' orphanage, and they were so beautiful and precious, my heart was full of love for them immediately. They had moved the girls off of the second floor for us to stay. We had been told to pack sheets and to make sure we had a top sheet. The fact we would need a top sheet in a tropical place seems a bit surprising, but I had done so. When we got to our room, one of the girls we were travelling with pulled out a can of bug spray, no one had told us to do that. The girls told us that we would want the sheet over us at night so that if a cockroach fell from the ceiling it would land on the sheet and not us. *Greaaaat*, I thought. As I looked around, I realized that there were plenty of windows, but they had neither glass nor screens. We decided to get our beds put together, and I made the mistake of looking at the bottom of my mattress, and yes outdoors lived inside, with not a family but an entire city of roaches living on the bottom of my mattress. That one can of bug spray would not take care of all of these, so we strategically sprayed around the edges of the mattresses we were going to sleep on, hoping the invisible barrier would be enough to keep them on their side of the line. We got ready for bed, and as I laid there in the dark, real dark, not like we have in America with all our streetlights, I thanked God for this opportunity and for the awareness and change I could feel in my own heart. Then I was brought back to reality when I felt a little plop on my sheet. Oh, no! One of those disgusting bugs had fallen on my sheet. One of the things I was shocked by were the variety of sizes, from normal to gigantic, that these roaches came in, and by the weight and feel, that one was pretty good size. It was not long before the girls next to me were making noises, more like groans as they were having the same sensation of falling roaches on their sheets. But as I laid there, I heard something else, it was the soft whispers and giggles of little girls. Yes, we were being pranked. The girls were throwing paper wads on us. We turned on the lights and had a good laugh, and they got scolded. But, in their defense, it was so worth it for the fun they had. We, these pampered American girls, were out of our element, and it was a good thing to be, out of our element. It is a place that God can speak to us, a place of heightened senses and a break from the trappings of routine and normal that tends to lull us into a trance. This was the first time I experienced life at its fullest, I sensed what being fully alive meant.

The next day, we went out to the church and started our VBS program, and we started promptly, on time, only to discover that people came and went as they pleased. At first, I was a little offended at their lack of punctuality, but then I realized that these people did not have clocks; their lives were not driven by that sense of urgency to get to the designated spot at a designated time. It was this kind of organic life that had a calm and a peace about it. Another culture rift in which the Lord was speaking to me through, kind of a Mary-Martha thing; maybe they were choosing a better way.

They took us back and forth from the boys' home for meals so we could eat together, and one of the first meals we had was a curry dish and rice and beans. We had the same thing most meals. It was fairly tasty, and I was a little shocked to find out we were eating curried goat. The real shock came when I realized that we were eating the boys' pet goat. It saddened me that they had to give up their pet for us to have food to eat, it was very humbling to say the least.

That was only one of the times we were humbled. We would get up early and get our showers before we left for the day. The shower was a pipe coming out of a concrete stall with a little window near the top, no glass, just a hole for light, which I might have seen if it was after sunrise. These were the quickest showers of my life, less than three minutes. The speed in which I showered was multipurpose: first, water was a precious commodity which was not always available; second, wherever the water came from it was really cold, like painfully cold; and third was that the concrete stall was pitch black and, after seeing the underside of the mattress, I cringed to think what might be in there with me.

One day, we arrived back at the orphanage to buckets, tubs, bowls, and bottles of water sitting around. The water had gone off, and the girls knew "how important it was to us" to take a shower every day, so they had walked to a well, working all day carrying back every container in the house with water so we could bathe. Sacrifice lived out for us. We all felt terrible that we had given the impression that we could not handle being a little sweaty and dirty. We were again humbled by their love.

During the evenings, we would venture higher up into the mountain to visit other villages and churches to worship together. There is something very holy and special about worshiping together with people of different cultures, again a glimpse of God's desire and heart for all people to live in unity in Him, and a glimpse of heaven. The time went way too quickly, and my mind was overwhelmed by the beauty and simplicity of life there.

There was a joy that they had that I did not see in America, and yet they had nothing. Or was I wrong? Maybe they had something better than things. I came feeling sorry for their physical poverty, and I left feeling sad for our culture in which most people live in a spiritual poverty. In reality, they were the ones most richly blessed. I believe that is why the scriptures warn about gaining the whole world and losing our soul. That is why I believe every American Christian needs to be stretched beyond their comfort zone, to experience something you cannot put into words, which changes the lens you see life with.

was the challenge I needed, a part of the testing and refining to see if I trusted God. I was not on this journey alone, and I knew it! My soul flourished at college, and I remember walking across campus praising and thanking God for allowing me to be at this place at this time, I had an unexplainable joy and peace, in spite of the intensity of school.

There was another college class that would change the direction of my life, Psychology 101. It might not surprise you, but I have always been a front-row person; I don't want to miss anything, and there are less distractions in the front row. I was serious about my education and was there to learn as much as I could. My friend Angela was of the same mindset and sat next to me at the table. It was a fairly large class, and I did not look behind me very often. I did know my friend Patty sat in the back row, she was an art student and was taking the class only because it was a required part of our liberal arts education.

One day, our professor let us go outside on the lawn for class. During his lecture, I heard a deep voice ask a very insightful question, and I had to see who asked such an intelligent question. When I looked around, I saw this very handsome guy with blue-green eyes, long eyelashes, curly brown hair, and he was built like a football player. (I had a thing for football players.) Why hadn't I noticed this guy before?

Well, the semester was drawing near it's end when Ang's sister came for a visit, and she came to our Psychology class. I insisted she take my seat, and I looked for another vacant seat in the room; there was one next to my friend Patty, in the row of art students. On the other side of me was the young man who I was surprised by. Yep, he was tall and handsome and a football player.

The professor handed back a test that day, and he saw my grade, and was shocked. It was an A, and this was a very difficult class, he asked me how I pulled that grade off. I chuckled and said I studied. His response was that he needed to study with me then. I often tutored people struggling in a class, so I told him he was welcome to come study with me for the final exam which was happening the day after next. He seemed surprised that I was serious, and we set a time for him to come over.

Now the timing was not great, Cindy had driven two hours to come see me for just a couple of days, and she had to hang out with one of my college friends while I tried to help this fellow student study. When he arrived, we started talking, and before I knew it, open dorm hours were over and he had to leave, and we had barely done any studying.

From our conversation, I had learned a lot about his family and him. After he left, I ran down to get Cindy, and I burst into the room announcing I wanted to marry a guy just like this Eric I had just spent a few hours conversing with.

The next day, we took our exam. He did not fare any better after our "study" session than he would have without it. After the exam, he stopped by to let me know that his father had called and asked him to skip the last month, our flex semester, so he could get down to Texas to help him with his construction business. He said he did not want me to think he just disappeared. He said he would be driving straight through, so I thought a care package with fresh fruits and snacks was in order. When I gave him the basket, he said he would be back early for football, and I told him I would be back early for student government and our annual RA (resident assistant) training. We agreed to look for each other then. He has been known to tell people the only thing he got out of Psychology 101 was me. He is so sweet.

We did catch up when we got back to school, and we had our first date on September 1. We were engaged by November 1 and announced it to his family at Thanksgiving. We announced it to my family on December 1. We planned a May 26 wedding—the weekend right after school was done. Of course, I called Cindy right away and told her the good news and told her to save the date. When Cindy called in February or March to tell me she was engaged too, she said they had set the date for May 26. When I told her that was our date, she laughed and said she knew the date sounded familiar. They were not able to accommodate a change, so we ended up changing our date to the twenty-seventh, the Indianapolis 500 Sunday, a real test of love for his family who were consummate race day attendees and fans.

Before I knew it, it was time to apply for physical therapy school. You could apply after three years or four. I was definitely hoping for the three plus two-and-a-half-year plan. I did not want to have to take that extra year if I didn't have to. Then they told us that there were over six hundred applicants for the twenty-eight positions. Grades, experience, and an interview would be the process to get accepted. They would only interview one hundred, but since I had done my undergraduate work there, I was automatically granted an interview. Once this process was completed, it was the waiting game. They would be sending us letters, with either the good news or the bad. We had been told that several hundred applicants had 4.0 GPAs. That made me nervous since we know that chemistry kept that from ever being a reality. This was such a stressful time, I was getting married in a matter of a week, and we would be heading to Austin, Texas.

The letter came days before we were done with school, and I was thirty out of six hundred. I did not make it in, I was the second alternate. My heart sank, Lord I have worked so hard and I have been faithful and I trust you, what is going on? I had opened the letter as soon as I got into the dorm, so I was standing by the door when I read the letter. My eyes welled up, and I turned and looked out the door, and sure enough there was a rainbow. That instant, I knew it was okay. As I prayed and asked God why He didn't let me get in as number twenty-eight. It was because it was about Him and not me. If I had just automatically gotten in, I would have thought I had earned it, rather than it being by His grace. It is always about His grace and glory, not about us. Within a week or so, I received notice that I was in, but I already knew it was going to be okay. God keeps His promises, always.

Chapter Four

New Chapter

Did I make it sound like life was smooth and easy after that? Well, it was not. It is not designed to be since the fall, back in the Garden of Eden. We are engaged in a battle, there is an enemy seeking to destroy and devour. Fortunately, the God we serve is bigger than our enemy.

We left Indiana to head to Texas so my husband could help his dad build houses in the Austin area. We arrived at his dad's house before him, as he and a friend named Walt had stayed back in Indiana to spend time with my mother-in-law and their family.

Well, my new father-in-law had moved down to the Austin area when there was a building recession in the Midwest. What he found when he arrived was that this was where he was meant to be, he felt he was finally home. He had a big heart and had taken in a homeless man who was a hard worker, but he could not manage money or caring for himself. As much as he loved his wife and family, stubbornness on both parts never allowed their family to live together in the same place again.

Well, I may have looked like a girly girl, but I was tougher than I looked. When I walked into the house outside Austin, where we would spend our first couple of summers in, I discovered what was meant when you say bachelor's pad. They had not completed the house, there were no cabinets and no kitchen sink; there was a ply-

play football in the fall, throw discus in the spring, go to school full time and work nights so we would have income and insurance.

When I was in my last year of graduate school, I discovered we had a surprise coming. If I did not complete my last class, I would have to wait another year to graduate. The way it worked out the last school year we had a certain number of courses, a certain number of weeks of internships, two weeks off and six weeks to finish our final class before graduation in mid-December. We could schedule our two weeks when we wanted, as long as it worked out for our internships, so I scheduled my two weeks off right before the last six weeks of class, and thankfully, that gave me two weeks to have our first child before I had to be in class.

One of my internships was in a pediatric rehabilitation center for the severe and profoundly handicapped. Pediatrics was one of my specialties, and I was excited to work with my pediatric professor. It ended up being an emotionally trying time for me, being pregnant and hearing all of the stories of the children I was working with. Many were related to birthing complications, and even though I was very healthy and had no problems during my pregnancy, it weighed heavy on me to see these precious children in what felt like hopeless situations for them and their families. By the time the rotation was done, I decided I could not do solely pediatrics and stay emotionally healthy.

When it was time for my first baby to be born, I was nervous and excited to see what God had for us. He was in no hurry and decided to wait a week to show up, leaving me one week before returning to classes.

During labor and delivery, I heard the nurses and doctor discussing issues which were going on, such as his positioning being wrong to deliver him, meconium staining, meaning the baby was in distress and had the first bowel movement before he was born, and it is a thick tarry stool that there was the potential for it to be aspirated or breathed in on his first breath (this was what had been the issue for one of the little guys I had worked with), then when I started pushing, the doctor said the cord was around his neck twice (one of the birth traumas of another one of the little guys I worked with), they had to use forceps to deliver him due to his very large head (another one of children had brain damage from the misuse of forceps).

Once he was delivered, they measured his head and they had concern that he might have hydrocephalus (a condition where there is a buildup of cerebrospinal fluid in the brain and which, if not treated with a shunt to drain the fluid, brain damage occurs). His initial testing results (APGARS) were not good. It had been a perfect pregnancy and everything which could go wrong seemed to be happening, this is when too much knowledge can be a bad thing. In those times, you have to trust God's plan.

We had dedicated this baby to the Lord Jesus at the moment we knew he existed, surrendering our rights to him. This was God's baby, and I had to trust Him. God's provision was already in place before I went into labor. The obstetrician I had delivering my baby had been delivering babies for forty years, he also was the doctor training the IU medical students how to do all the procedures and techniques he had to use on my baby. I fully believe that anyone less experienced would not have been able to handle his birth without causing permanent damage.

They monitored his head circumference for several months and came to the conclusion he just had a large cranium. How we celebrated when he would come home from elementary and middle school with straight As and at the top of the scale for the annual standardized testing, knowing how his story could be so different.

God protected him for a purpose, and when I look at what a sensitive, caring, loving and godly man of integrity he has turned out to be, I thank the Lord. Even if things had not turned out so well, God would have deserved our praise because He always uses what satan intends for harm for our good. He told us that, and you can trust Him. I trust Him.

Chapter Five

Real Life

Graduate school was finished and we moved to Danville, Indiana, to Eric's hometown. I had done an internship there, and they had a great hospital in which both his mother and sister worked in. We lived there about two years, and it was a blessing to be a part of the community in which he grew up and meet and get to know the significant people in his life. It also allowed me to get to know his family on a much deeper level than I would have otherwise. It also allowed his family to bond with Austin. Eric's mom was the one who watched him while I worked. she was a third-shift nurse, and she would nap when he did and sleep when I got home. Those were special times for us.

Eric's career was a more difficult journey. When he graduated from college with a degree in commercial art and graphic design, computers were just entering the workflow of the art world. It was a little disheartening getting your foot in the door. He had a couple of times he was applying for jobs paying four dollars an hour, and there would be a line around the block of people with bachelor's degrees in art looking for their break. God had a plan, and his high school art teacher was going on an extended leave; she called and asked Eric to sub for her for the semester. He is a great teacher and loved having that opportunity. That then ended at the perfect time to work for a new company, which was taking artwork and converting it to be input in a computer for embroidery. That job gave him experience working on computers with art and design. That then opened the door for him to work for a company learning how to use graphic design programs on computers so he could teach companies how to use the software effectively. One of the first companies he trained was a Fortune 500 company. They were so impressed with him that they asked him to be their trainer in the use of graphic design software in their print shop. It was a great opportunity, but it would require our relocating.

It coincided with the pending birth of our second child, Sierra. She was absolutely beautiful, and her delivery was much less complicated than the first. I was looking forward to a longer maternity leave than the week I had with my first. It was a few days after delivery, Eric was already commuting to his new job two hours away, when I thought maybe I should be checking out the career opportunities in the Batesville area, where we were moving to. The community was a beautiful quaint small town of 3,800, nestled in southeastern Indiana, with only one hospital.

I had decided I would look for a job once we moved there; enjoying this new baby was my priority. Somehow, on this particular day, I sensed I needed to call this hospital and at least make a contact. So I did. The lady I spoke to said she could not believe my timing. They did need a physical therapist, and they had been looking for some time for a director of Physical Therapy. She was getting ready to call someone within the hour and offer the job to them, but after speaking with me, she really wanted to interview me before making her decision, could I please come and interview in the next couple days as she did not want to put off the other person too long.

Arrangements were made for me to go interview after less than a week after Sierra was born. They offered me the job on the spot but needed me to start immediately. I negotiated two more weeks, as we had to finish packing and get physically moved. God had once again directed and opened a door. He also gave me a peace and bandwidth to be a working mom. Because it was the call on my life to do both, He supernaturally allowed it to work. As I look back, I believe what God was requiring of me was to keep my will and life surrendered to Him. It could not just be about what I wanted. It was about being put in a position to have to trust Him but continually seeing Him showing up in small and big ways.

My new job was interesting. I was the director of myself and an aide that worked there, and we had one small room in the basement to work out of. It was my responsibility to treat the inpatients, outpatients, the skilled nursing-home patients in the tower, and to do the therapy for home health care over a very large two-county area. Once there was some continuity in therapy, it took off. Soon, we needed a secretary to answer all the phone calls, as the aide was spending more time on the phone than being able to help transport and set up for patients. It was a time there was a severe shortage of therapists, and we received many recruiter phone calls trying to find bodies to fill vacant positions, and just keeping them at bay was almost a full-time job. It was not long before we outgrew our space and needed additional therapists, and we were able to expand our services. As the hospital saw things growing, they were willing to invest in state-of-the-art equipment and do some shuffling to give us more space.

We loved the area and began making long-term plans to stay there. It was scenic, with amazing people, great jobs, and both Eric and I were moving along in our careers. It was a great place to raise a family. Being a couple of hours away from his family and three hours away from mine seemed to be the only negative. Fortunately, we had Eric's brother Nick and his wife, Kelly, who lived in Cincinnati, and we could visit them more often. We also had our third child, Marshall, while we lived in Batesville. It all seem to have come together in the over three years we had lived there.

One day, my secretary had headed out to lunch just before me, and the phone rang as I was going out the door. I debated whether to answer it, but decided I should. It was a recruiter; at least he introduced himself as such, which they often did not do. He also said he was trying to find a therapist for northern Indiana. Well, one of my therapists was from northwestern Indiana and had expressed a desire to move back there to watch her nieces and nephews grow up, so I listen longer than I had ever done. Much to my surprise, he told me he was recruiting for a small town in northern Indiana, for a hospital called Wabash County Hospital. Really? I laughed out loud, and he asked why that was funny and if I had ever heard of it. When I told him it was the town in which I grew up in, he asked if I was interested in moving back. Without hesitation, I said no, but I would speak to some colleagues and see if any were looking to relocate. So I took his name and number and went ahead and met my husband for lunch.

When I told Eric about this funny situation, he didn't laugh; he told me to call and schedule an interview. He informed me that we didn't believe in coincidences, and so we needed to pay attention. It was true. Out of the literally thousands of recruiter phone calls which came through that department, for me to pick up and listen to the one recruiting for my hometown was more than coincidental. I called and scheduled an interview.

When I met with the Human Resources director and the hospital vice president, they asked what it would take to turn the department around. Since I did not want the job, I did not hold back, listing all the equipment they would need to purchase and things which would need to be addressed. It was a long drive home. After driving almost three and a half hours, my husband was shocked at how bad I looked, with a mottled and blotchy face with makeup runs. He said it looked as though I cried all the way home, and I had.

He really expected it to go better than that. He asked what had happened, and I explained that they had offered me the job. It puzzled him as to why that was so upsetting, when he knew we had always agreed to go where God lead. My heart wanted to be obedient, and I knew I was playing a tug of war I could not win. I really was willing to go wherever God called, but God knew the one place I really did not want to go to, the one exception to total surrender, so of course He had to challenge it. If He didn't, He would not be able to do with me in the future what He wanted. It was a necessary discipline. His will was obvious, and I was serious about being obedient, but he let me grieve the plans we had made, which would not come to pass, the careers and people we loved that we would be leaving, and of course, my will which I had to surrender again.

It was beyond comprehension that we would leave due to my career. Eric's career as a graphic designer would be a much harder fit in a small town, and we had mentally prepared to move based on the opportunities God opened for him. But for my career to be the precipitator for the move did not make sense in human terms, but I did trust God and His heart for me and for my family. I wanted this move to be a good thing for Eric also, so God made it easier on me with a great opportunity for Eric, at least while we made plans and I headed up to start work. I had been back for a few weeks when Eric was heading up to start his new job doing art for NFL teams, something he was excited about, but they rescinded the offer two days before he was to start due to having to let seventeen artists go.

It did not take long for another opportunity to arise in which he was able to set up his dream office and purchase all the hardware and software he preferred, which allowed him to step into the world of the Mac, which he knew would be the way of the future in graphic design and photography.

Moving back to my hometown has been such a blessing. Wow, God knew best. Over the years, we have been able to renew relationships, my children have been able to know my parents and family in a way they never would have if we still lived three to four hours away. I believe it has been a blessing for my parents also.

We also have been able to invest in our church. When we were dating, Eric came to my home church and loved it. He was raised Catholic, and he found the setting and worship in the Friends church very fulfilling, so one of the wins with the move was coming back to be a part of this growing vibrant church. It was very refreshing and allowed us to grow in ways we had not in our other church settings.

Chapter Six

Parenting

There are many challenges being parents, balancing time with each other, investing time with each child, with the family, and the extended family. When my first three were little and about two years apart, it was a different kind of chaos than I had ever experienced before, one I was struggling to handle.

Having made the choice to nurse each child for their first year, because research had shown that to be critical for their well-being, I had to fit in extra feedings during the night to make up for working during the day. So from the time my first was nearing his due date until now, I can count on my fingers the number of full night's sleep I have gotten. Of course, now it is not feeding babies that is waking me up but a byproduct of having all those babies.

Being a perfectionist by nature and being raised by a stay-at-home mother, the bar was set pretty high. Order and cleanliness are things which give me peace and a sense of well-being. I was finding it increasingly difficult to keep all the plates spinning. Work was going well, and we had added staff, but also responsibilities. When I came home, I wanted to have time with the kids and to keep things in order. With two busy and one nonmobile, I was still spinning plates pretty well. Once I got them all down for the night, I had two to three hours to reclaim the house and spend a little time with my husband, who I love being with.

Number three did not stay nonmobile, and our house was big enough and had two levels. I could not be everywhere at once, and therefore, plates spun out of control. I would be in one place entertaining a child or two, and one would wander off and create a mess, like emptying the closet I just reorganized or throwing Cheerios all over. Previously, silence was golden; it is when I hear the Lord the best. All of a sudden, silence was my enemy. If things were quiet, one, two, or potentially three children were up to no good. If they were crying or fussing with each, you knew that at that moment they were all alive. It is truly by His grace that He sustained me.

There was, however, a day—I cannot remember the date—but the day I remember vividly. I was upstairs refolding the towels that number three had pulled out of the linen closet for the umpteenth time, when there was silence downstairs in the family room; it's never a good sign. I ran down to find that I had new murals on three walls and two very adorable but guilty children staring at me with the deer in headlights eyes. They knew better, you could tell by their expression, it was as if they were trying to break me.

Well, that day, it worked. I had a proverbial meltdown. Going to the top of the steps, I sat down and just sobbed. I cried out to the Lord and said, "I cannot do it . . . I cannot keep everything perfect." Then I heard the Lord speak to me, not audibly, but just as clear as if it were, "Who expects you to? Not me." What? I asked. The scripture in Colossians 3:23 about whatever you do, do it as if unto the Lord, not man. Doesn't that mean perfection?

As I thought through this revelation, if God does not expect perfection, who does? It certainly was not my husband expecting it. You mean this has been self-inflicted? The Lord let me know I was at a critical point. I could continue on this impossible path seeking an unattainable perfection, which would drive me and my precious family crazy, or I could seek the better things. It was time to make a choice; was I going to be a Mary or a Martha?

The decision was easy and difficult at the same time. I did decide to let go and chill out. And if anyone would look at my house today, they would say I relaxed a little too much. It has been a decision I have never regretted, and unless I get out of balance myself,

I choose to invest my time and energy into my family and people. When my house and things start getting to me, I know something is out of whack, and it is time to pray through what the source of the stress is.

In the middle of those years, we had a miscarriage, which any woman understands is a difficult process. Truthfully, it seems the not getting to know them and to see their potential lived out here with us is the hardest. You know in your heart they are fine, they just got to bypass the struggles of life and make it to the final destination on the express flight. It is our loss that we grieve. I must say in the most difficult times of my life, the peace of Christ has been tangible. I am so thankful for His presence in my life.

There are also those special treasures you hold close to your heart. One of those was when I had been put on bed rest during this miscarriage. Marshall was almost four. He came running into my bedroom jubilant. He said that he had just had a dream, but he wasn't really asleep. He was sitting on his bed when an angel came down and was holding our baby. The voice was so soft and sweet, and it was so bright. The angel said God was letting him see and hold the baby so he would know that she was okay. So, he held her very carefully, and then the angel told him that it was time to go and they needed to go back to heaven. So, the angel took the baby back in its arms and went back up into the sky. He knew he was the first one to see her and that just blessed him. It blessed me also.

It was about a year later that we had our fourth baby, Faith Anastasia. She came five weeks early, but was due on Easter. Anastasia means resurrection or rebirth. The name was beautiful and meaningful on several levels. It is a reminder of how God takes us out of the valleys and offers hope and renewal.

Faith was also the name of a dear lady in our lives. She was a patient of mine several years prior, who, when I met her, I knew was going to be a challenge. She was very direct and loud. She had been through the maze of healthcare and was not happy she was being sent to one more place. She had no use for therapy, and she did not want to be there. And I believe everyone within a city block was aware of how she felt pretty quickly.

Remember I love a challenge; well, one had walked right into my department. After sitting and listening to her situation and evaluating her, I assured her we would be able to help her, and if we didn't, she did not have to come back. One of the blessings the Lord has blessed me with is to hear what is not being said, the backstory, the deeper things. Within a few sessions, she had gone from being one of the most difficult patients ever to one of our favorites. She just needed to know someone cared about her, her story, her sadness, and her disappointments.

Years later, she was still stopping by baking things for the entire department and visiting. She was one of the people I cried about leaving behind. She loved children and worked in a school lunchroom to be near them. One of her greatest sorrows was to never be able to have children. When I called and told her that we had just had our fourth child and we named her Faith, she just wept. I do not believe anything else could have blessed her more. She said the most interesting thing when she met our Faith; she said she would never do anything to dishonor the name they shared. How I loved that lady, and so did God.

Chapter Seven

Counter Cultural

There have been many other things we have been intentional about when it has come to our children, some of which have not been fully appreciated by them at the time. There have been crazy things which may not be a big deal to others but were to me, like holidays. It has always been important to me that my children know that I would never lie to them, not even a "white lie" or a culturally accepted falsehood, which was meant to create fun for kids. There has been more than once that my mother has disagreed with me and told me so.

When it came to Santa, I did not want anything Santa Claus in my home, and I never told my children there was a Santa. It has always been completely about the birth of Christ. I wanted them to know what was real and what was not. I wanted them to know they can trust me to always tell them truth. The funny thing was we never told them anything about Santa, but they heard it so much from those around them that they assumed it was true. Typically, within a few years, they would ask if he was real, and I would tell them about St. Nicholas who was a godly man who did kind acts for children, and the legend grew from there. I explained that over the years, many people started forgetting about Jesus, so that was why we choose not to highlight Santa.

Halloween was another celebration I struggled with. The first couple of years, we dressed the kids in cute outfits and took them around, but something within me did not feel good about just participating in a day that was steeped in evil traditions and threats. We then did not participate for a couple of years. Then I remembered the saying "All it takes for evil to win is for good men to do nothing," and I thought about how that applied to Halloween. We then decided to go on the offensive; instead of "trick or treat," we would "treat or treat." We would take goodies or roses to people who were not able to get out of their homes much, and for several years, I would pen a poem about why we chose to "treat or treat." The kids could dress up as good characters, but it was our goal to bless others, not to expect anything. Now more times than not, they come home with a bag or lap of goodies themselves, but that is not the focus. That tradition continues at our house.

Another area we were intentional about was entertainment. Now that was not to say we have not run into issues where we have gone to see a movie or sit to watch a show that we didn't end up regretting it. That decision was not just for our children, that was for us too. If it is not suitable for them, it was probably not suitable for us either.

I came to that conclusion after a specific event, one in which some might not think too much about, but for me, it rocked my world. At work, we would listen to Christian CDs most of the time, and if someone got tired of hearing those, they would put on the radio. I was fine with that; it seemed like a good compromise, until I was setting a patient up on a piece of exercise equipment and there was this melodic ballad which came on, great music, a song by Bread, I believe. Before I knew it, I was singing the lyrics. I did not memorize them, I had never really paid attention to the words, and then I realized the words coming out of my mouth were "I sing to the god of sex, drugs and rock-n-roll." WHAT? How could those words leave my mouth? They are so contrary to my heart! Immediately, I denounced those words and turned off the radio. Music has a way of breaking through our conscious mind and is taken in on a deeper level. When I think about how music influences my mood and thoughts, I made the personal decision that I did not want anything else played in my car or home than music which draws me closer to the Lord, or is uplifting and encouraging.

When we moved to Wabash, we stayed with my parents while we looked for a home, and during that time we slept on a sleeper sofa. My dad would watch shows as I was trying to go to sleep, and he did not pay attention to the vocabulary on the shows he watched. I would cringe at some of the language, but I was a guest in his home, and it seemed inappropriate to tell my father what was okay to watch. During that time, though, I started to have words of profanity pop into my mind as I would be driving or feeling a little stressed. As I prayed about it, I realized that even though I was not paying attention to those shows and the dialogue, my mind, like a sponge, was picking up those words, which I would never say or want exposed to. There are spiritual forces at work in all aspects of our lives, and darkness seeks to influence us when we are not diligent in guarding our hearts and minds. So it is not surprising that we have chosen to be careful about what we listen to and what we watch. Sources such as Plugged-In and Screen-It were valuable in reviewing content to protect ourselves from unwanted garbage. The saying "garbage in, garbage out" is more true than we realize. Unfortunately, with the advent of smartphones and computers for every student, it has gotten harder to monitor it all. We have tried to build the case with all of our children about the importance of protecting themselves.

I know that there have been some triumphs. When my boys have gone with friends and when the group changed the movie when they got there or when the language took a turn, they got up and walked out and waited for their friends in the lobby. As young adults, I do not know if they have maintained that level of diligence or not; if not, I hope that the Holy Spirit works to protect them and, when necessary, convict them.

One of our and the students favorite lesson series when teaching middle school Sunday school was on entertainment. Eric would review the top TV shows, movies, and songs for the year and review and break down some of the content. It was appalling how many words of profanity could be in one show. One movie ninety minutes long had ninety-two "bomb" words, just that one word alone. It doesn't take much writing skill if 50 percent of the words are profanity and expletives.

Sometimes, after reading the lyrics of the top songs, he would act like he was going to read them in class, and you could see the kids recoil, as they knew what would be coming. As a part of the series, usually toward the end, I would bake chocolate-chip cookies, and we would pass them around, kids excited and chowing down. Eric would go into the spiel about how picky I am about my ingredients when I bake, the best flour, sugar, real butter, real chocolate chips, and a little dog poop. Not much mind you, just a little. A little poop won't kill you, will it? The kids always make faces and stop eating their cookies. Then Eric says, "When you watch shows or listen to music with foul language, it is filth that gets on you. Yes, there may be some good things in a song or show, but how much 'poop' do you want to wade through to get to the few good things, and how much sticks to you? Wouldn't you prefer cookies without the poop? Then maybe we need to avoid it in other things." Of course, in reality, there was no dog poop; it was merely an analogy to get their attention.

Praying about what God wants you to do in life cannot be overstated. God's plans and purposes are different in different lives. You need to seek what He wants for you and your family. When Austin was starting kindergarten, we debated about Christian school, homeschooling, or public school. As with most things in our marriage, we will typically pray together, then pray separately about a situation and then come together for confirmation. This is what we did about what setting our children would be educated.

Now, with the intentionality of how we were raising our children, public school would not have been our first choice. We had worked hard at nurturing and protecting our children, and we did not relish the idea of that being undone. The Lord convicted us both that our children were to go to public school. I sensed the Lord saying that if all the parents who are being intentional about how they raise their children keep them from the public arena, who will be there to be a light?

For our family, we knew that they needed to learn how to deal with the real world and real struggles that other kids went through.

My spirit understood this was the training ground for where God was going to take them later. Even knowing this was where God wanted them, there were days that I would ask God, "Are you sure about this?" I remember Austin as a kindergartner being bullied and made to lick the bus floor. I was furious, but it was an opportunity to teach. We discussed why that was wrong, and I told him to remember how it felt to be picked on by bigger kids or mean kids and to never let that happen to another kid when he was one of the bigger boys. We talked about how sad it was that those kids did not have anyone teaching them about right and wrong and that was an opportunity to pray for them. Or when Sierra was in kindergarten and I was in the car driving with her. I was talking about her dad and I going out on a date that night, and my beautiful innocent daughter said matter of factly, "That is so you can have sex, right?" WHAT? I remember the absolute disbelief that this just came from my little girl. Another teaching moment. Upon further discussion, she said that was what the teenagers on the bus said. So I explained that was not the purpose of a date, it was to spend time getting to know someone or to get to have time to talk and never was the purpose of a date to have sex. Sex was reserved for marriage, and it was something very special, a gift from God, not something to be cheapened like that. Later, we moved into a different school district, and I was shocked and humbled by the response of the principal and several teachers, who were sincerely saddened, and a few with tears, that they would not get to have all the Schoening kids because they had been a blessing and they made a difference. Thank you, Lord.

Our kids would be the first to tell you we were not perfect, but they do know our hearts, and what we live in public is what we live at home. In a world that likes to compartmentalize everything, it is a dangerous game in the world of faith. One of the biggest criticisms I have heard over the years is the stumbling block that people create when they are one thing in church, another at work, another with friends, and another at home or with family. Those who claim to be Christians but compartmentalize and justify this inconsistency have hurt the witness and name Christian and have become the excuse

Chapter Eight

Dreams and Visions

Throughout the Bible, you read about God communicating to people in dreams. Many have thought that was a thing of the past. Then there are those who try to find meaning in every dream. Many dreams seem to be bits of our day, things we are processing and trying to make sense of; but there are spiritual dreams. It should not surprise us that God reveals Himself in these ways. The Bible gives many examples of God using these means, and it tells us that God will use them more and more in the end times. When you think of Joseph and his dreams, you know the foretelling of a family and a nation's future; the dreams of kings in which God used the gift of interpreting dreams to open doors and build influence in throne rooms, such as He did with Joseph and Daniel. In Numbers 12:6, it says the Lord reveals Himself to the prophets in dreams and visions. In Acts 2:17, it says, "In the last days, God says, I will pour out my Spirit on all people, your sons and daughters will prophesy, your young men will see visions, your old men will dream dreams." Did you catch that? God says He will pour out His Spirit on ALL people. Why does it seem many in the body of Christ seem to discount or be fearful of dreams and visions? What does not acknowledging these gifts result in?

God speaks to me in dreams. Yep, I said it; it is now out there for all to see. He will also whisper things to me at the break of day, as I am praying my day into place. I think it is because I get in the way less during the night when I am quiet and less distracted. When I am awake fully, my mind wants to take me to fifty places at once. And when my mind is racing and distracted, I cannot seem to listen as well. Typically, God uses dreams and visions to get my attention, give me direction, to teach me a spiritual truth, or give me a warning. Dreams given to me by God are vivid, and it is about the details, the fact that I am mentally and spiritually aware and engaged in them, and the fact that they stay with me. The visions and dreams the Lord has given me can be pulled up in my mind to study and ponder, they don't go away. I don't remember ever having a dream change, but my visions do. The way God uses dreams and visions in my life has grown and changed as I step more and more in obedience.

For me, a vision is connected to a prayer assignment, and if I accomplish what the purpose of the vision was, I see it change. It is partially how God wired me; I love mysteries and putting clues together and to be able to be used by God is the best thing in the universe. Now, I don't tell everyone about this, well not until now, but it is time. For many, this may seem like crazy talk, but I hope you will finish reading about some of my adventures so that you might be encouraged at how God is alive and active in our lives if we are willing to take steps of faith and be obedient. It is time for others who have gifts that the Holy Spirit has given them to better understand them and why they have them, to empower those that God is calling to step into The Story in ways you have never imagined, to be willing to go where God calls you.

Back to my dream about humbling myself. It is one of the earliest spiritual dreams I remember having. In my dream, my husband and I pulled up to the edge of a large parking lot and there were rows and rows of noble African warriors all standing at attention; they all were wearing white, black, and red. They looked like they were waiting for someone to lead them, and they were facing toward us. They held long spears in their hands. Then there was a building, and at the front door stood warriors on either side, guarding who could come and go, and there was one warrior standing facing me, spear in hand. I approached him, and he asked if I wanted to enter and be used by God. My answer was an immediate yes, and I stepped closer to the door. He stepped in front of me to cut me off. It caught me off guard that he kept me from being able to enter the door. He then looked and nodded just behind me, and there was a fenced kennel-type area with a little doggy door, and it had dog poop on the ground. I looked back at him, and he nodded back at me like that was the way I had to get into the building. Literally, I had to get on my hands and knees and be willing to crawl through dog business to get to the little door. I remember thinking, you have to be kidding. Then I heard it, "If you want to be used by Me, you have to be willing to humble yourself," then I woke up.

That dream was years and years ago, but I remember it to the detail, like a video I can play back at my leisure. I have prayed about that dream many times, and want to be willing to go and do whatever God calls me to, just to have a chance to be used.

God speaks to me too. Now, I know that even sounds crazier than the dreams thing, but it is true. I personally have never heard an audible voice with my ears; I see words in my head or hear a phrase in my mind. God will give me a couple words or a short sentence that I have to pray about and figure out how it fits with my life. The first phrase I heard was "Abide in me." Seems like a simple phrase, but I have spent hours researching and praying over that phrase, trying to understand what God fully means by it. There was a season it came to me over and over, so I figured I was still not really getting it.

Just FYI, I think God may speak in King James. So many times, it seems that the phrases or scriptures I hear are in KJV. Just saying. He also has asked me to "feed his sheep," another one I have spent many hours trying to understand and make sure I am obedient about. Personally, it sounds like being a pastor, but I have never felt like that was my call. Over the years, though, I have had many patients who have come into the clinic, who need to be fed and encouraged and words of truth spoken into their lives. It is my privilege and calling to invest in that way with them. On my schedule, they just look like regular appointments, I call those divine appointments.

One of the ways he gives me a heads up that he is moving and how He gets me in tune is when I hear Him say, "Do you trust me?" I always get a little nervous when I start hearing that. My answer has always been yes. With everything and with every part of my being,

IT'S ABOUT HIM

I trust Him. It is me I don't trust. I always have to test my heart and motives. Often, it then will change to, "Are you ready?" Then I know to brace myself for something new, exciting and/or scary. Not fear kind of scary but anticipation, stretching kind of scary.

There have been times He has warned me He wants me to go to the dark places or the hard places. He has taken me there and revealed Himself over and over. Dark places and hard places have been where the enemy has a spiritual stronghold, oppressing believers, some of the unreached places in the world, or where lives seem trapped in hopelessness. Nations which claim they are Buddhist, Hindu, Muslim, are labeling themselves with words which have spiritual power and authority. They as nations are aligning themselves with darkness and don't realize it.

The Lord recently revealed to me something which seems obvious in some ways yet goes against the cultural norm in America—the belief and statement that we need to respect all religions because we all live in the same world. When I hear it, my spirit bristles. Finally, a couple of weeks ago, a friend and colleague made that statement, one I had heard a few times in a week. Suddenly, I could not hold it back and retorted, "No we don't." She turned and looked at me in disbelief that I had responded with that. It sounds so harsh and disagreeable, doesn't it? And we should know in our culture that it is unacceptable. I proceeded to say, "That is a lie." We have accepted this lie, and we don't mind because it takes the pressure off the need to evangelize.

If we acknowledge Christ as our savior and truly believe He is the way, the truth, and the life, then all those other religions are traps which have imprisoned millions of lives. Who set those traps? God? How absurd! Satan did. Why on earth would I respect institutions in which satan is leading lambs to slaughter—no worse, away from Christ. God does NOT call us to respect all religions; He calls us to LOVE ALL people! Let us not confuse the two and be complacent with the souls of our brothers and sisters in humanity, who are blind, broken, and trapped. Telling people they are okay when they are not is not love. Speaking truth, caring, praying for them, entering into their world with hope, that is love; that changes hearts and can transform our world.

Chapter Nine

The Battle

He has also asked me to "walk and pray," which first started at church and usually in the middle of the service. At first, I would feel bad leaving in the middle of a sermon, and I would try to wait it out, but I discovered God can get really loud in your head if you are not quick to listen and obey. So, He started calling me out to pray around our church nearly every Sunday. I had never done that kind of prayer walking before and didn't know what He was asking exactly, so I would pray for the pastor and church leaders, for wisdom, discernment, protection. Then I would pray for the people in church that their hearts and minds would be receptive to truth, that they would be protected from the schemes and plans of the enemy. That blinders would be removed, walls of deception to be broken down, spirits of fear to be bound, hardness of hearts to be softened. I would pray for those not there. I would pray that our church would be a safe haven, a place of renewal, encouragement, and blessing.

The first time I was called out to walk and pray, nearing the completion of my first lap, a pickup truck started to pull onto the church campus. It saw me, slammed on their brakes, spit on the ground, and took off. Then I realized for the first time that the enemy had our church in his sights. Whatever that truck planned was thwarted, and I prayed to break the curse they put on the church with their spitting on the ground. Sometimes, as I walked and prayed, specific names would come to mind to pray for or over. God told me He was calling me into something, and He required three things of me— "obedience, perseverance, and sacrifice."

God had appointed me as a watchman at our church. That was a new thing to me, and God took me to Ezekiel. It was my training ground for hearing and trusting the Lord in new ways. I would be called at all hours to go pray at the church, for the church, and for the spiritual battle that was raging over it. I saw a vision of a black cloak which was hung over the top of the church almost like a tent. As I walked and prayed, I prayed that God would loosen the binds which were trying to bring a spiritual darkness to our church. Over weeks and months of walking and praying, the vision changed; and eventually, the black cloak was replaced with the vision of a rainbow with sunny skies over our church. That was confirmation that the spiritual stronghold had been broken.

What I discovered was that a family I knew had taken a young mother and her child into their home. I had seen them and had spoken to the mother a few times. At that point, they were not telling anyone about her backstory, that they were trying to rescue her from a satanic cult into which she had been born. That was why the spiritual battle had heightened and why God was calling me out to pray and intercede in a battle I had not known existed but God knew.

It was a time when the bliss of ignorance was stolen away. Life was simpler and nicer not to know about how the enemy works and just how evil, evil is. Satan, in our culture, is the cartoon red devil with a pointy tail, more of a joke to dismiss than to really believe in or to fear, but this was a disturbing revelation. The young mother I will call Liz was attracted to me. She later told me she saw the light of Christ shining from my eyes, and so she knew I was safe. She had been ritually abused, programmed, and tortured to create a world of fear to control her and others. The occult prefers to stay in the shadows, where it is hard to identify. They really don't like being exposed, and having her there and protected made them nervous.

It became an all-consuming process to protect this girl and her child. It also became a burden and an expense. The woman of the couple who had taken her in had met her at a Bible study, and at one point, Liz reached out for help. Options were limited due to the severity of her abuse and the danger to her and her child, so she became a part of their family. It caused much stress and rifting in their family, and the isolation and stress took a toll on them all.

Eric and I were called to step in and help. My dreams and visions increased, and I began understanding how to help her. We would pray together and pray through the brainwashing and programming. Then we started being under more attack ourselves. It became the routine to wake up at 3:00 a.m. shaking, needing to pray and intercede for her or others or for my own family.

For those who doubt the reality of satan and his realm, trust me, he is real, and he is at work to destroy, deceive, divide, and steal away all he can. I remember one time awaking from a dream with Faith in the middle of a satanic ritual, and I woke Eric to go pray over the kids because they were in danger. I needed to stay and pray through the situation, I asked him to start in Faith's room.

He went upstairs, and when he walked into her room, he suddenly felt he had gotten clotheslined and was knocked to the floor on his back, with his head reeling. At six foot four inches, with 225 pounds of muscle, this was not some small feat. He immediately rebuked satan and claimed the blood of Christ over Faith, her room, and our home. He then proceeded to each of the other bedrooms to pray. I am not telling you this to create fear or to glorify satan. We don't want to focus on him, but we do need to understand he is real, that he has a plan and an agenda, and what we see with human eyes is only a fraction of what exists.

Have your ever thought about how amazing it is that cell phones exist and we can call, text, FaceTime, or Skype without any wires connecting our phones, tablets, or laptops, and we can do this to anywhere in the world? There is this invisible world of soundwaves, microwaves, short waves, radiation, etc., which we witness in action every day, and yet we are surprised or doubt the existence of the spiritual realm and the Creator of it all.

The power of Christ is greater than the enemy, but so many people in this world choose not to pick a side or to be engaged in the battle for souls. What people fail to realize, is that by not choosing actively, you still have made a choice, or one has been made for you. There are only three roles in this epic battle: those fighting for Christ, those fighting for satan, and the people who are victims of the darkness. That is it, plain and simple. The majority of the world lives in the middle ground, not understanding there is a battle; they being victims and being clueless about it.

God seeks to set the captives free, to loosen the chains and yokes holding people in bondage, but it takes warriors to intercede to set the captives free. I am one of those warriors, and I serve a mighty God who loves us with reckless abandon, and who grieves for lives destroyed and manipulated, hearts broken or hardened, those seeking wholeness in the world, and finding imitation lives without purpose, passion, or direction. I challenge you that being engaged and used to bless others is so much better than the alternative. Take that step of faith, be bold, love recklessly, speak truth and blessing into the lives of the people you come in contact with. Lives are transformed by the power of Christ released through prayer and caring for the lost in this world. We all are kingdom builders. Whose kingdom are you working on? If it is yours, you're on a fool's quest because only what is done for Christ will last. Truly. If you want to make a difference, leave a mark; but the only mark which matters is the cross.

One of the things I learned through this journey was just as it is my heart to bless, there are many who actively practice witchcraft by cursing those around them. When I pray to break any curses or works of darkness against myself or others, I always profess my forgiveness toward them, so that they are not bound by the evil they wished upon me or others. Forgiveness is what brings healing and freedom, so by willingly giving it, the perpetrators realize their work has been undone, and I pray that the Holy Spirit will let them know it is by the power of the living Christ that this is accomplished, to help draw them to Him. There is power in prayer, there is power in forgiveness. We must remember to use the tools Jesus has left us to claim what was stolen and lost.

There is power in words. God spoke the universe into existence. He used His words to create, to build up, to establish the physical world we live in. He also used words to instruct, encourage, reprimand, and direct the spiritual world and man. He is always intentional with His words.

He was also intentional about how he created man. Man is the only thing he created that He did not speak into existence. Have you ever wondered why he did not just speak us into existence? It is because He set man apart. Why did He set man apart? I believe it was because He wanted beings to be in charge and engaged in His kingdom, beings handpicked and formed to be unique. He wanted to empower us with the ability to make a difference, to bless, and edify His creation, including each other.

When sin entered into the picture, it not only resulted in mankind being expelled from Eden, but instead of our words being fed by the Tree of Life, they were now influenced by the fruit which came from the Tree of Knowledge of good and evil. It changed everything, including the way words were used. Now words could curse, wound, and destroy. Words uttered by man have a spiritual component. They affect the spiritual world and God's creation. That is why in Ephesians, it speaks of staying away from vulgar jokes and foul language. The spirit of God is not what is powering profanity and vulgarity, it is sin and darkness. That is why God wants us to guard our mouths, hearts, and minds.

When you look at a young child who has never heard words of hope, love, and grace, they are a shell of a human. Have you wondered why there is disconnect with so many youth? What words could have been used to fill them?

Just as God breathed His breath into man, he breathed power into our lungs to breathe out words, words in which He intended for good, words to heal, empowered words to transform lives. We need to be more intentional with how we use words. Do we think about the spiritual impact of our words? That is why prayer is so powerful, it is an unleashing of the breath of God through words. Prayer matters, words matter, people matter, they all connect back to the heart of God.

We, as followers of Christ, need to pay special attention to Christ's words, His prayer, and the Word. Within the power of words, we bless and connect to God, the power and source of it all. Remember there are three words God put into my life as I have walked and prayed asking to be used by Him: obedience, perseverance, and sacrifice.

Chapter Ten

Action Instead of Excuses

As noted in my story about my trip to Jamaica, missions has always been close to my heart because it is close to God's. Now I have had some interesting conversations from believers who believe we should not spend time and money on world missions. They say it is because there is so much need within our own country. What I have observed is that, often, these same Christians live their lives, not investing in the need here either. It is as if this conviction absolves them from being involved anywhere. Now many of these are the same people who have never really been beyond the borders of this country, maybe that is why their vision is so shortsighted. This is where I remind them that if God has convicted them of the need here, they had better be stepping into that to make a difference and not use it as the excuse to avoid investing beyond our borders.

The bottom line is we cannot afford to stay in our comfort zones. This reminds me of the Good Samaritan story we have all read in the Bible. I believe the message in that story was that we cannot define the world as us and them, like the Jews and Samaritans or the blacks and whites. We are all a part of the same world. As Christians, the body of Christ, when we see someone in need physically, emotionally, or spiritually, we are called, commanded to get involved. When we pass by a hurting wounded world, what we are telling the world is that we deserve to be born here and spend our lives seeking comfort and luxury, while you deserve to be born without, struggling for survival, but by the grace of God that could be us. We don't deserve any more than the least of these, and they don't deserve any less than what we have. If you don't understand that, you miss the point. We all are in desperate need of a savior and His grace.

It is the same unconscious mindset that says I am a Christian; I have my ticket into heaven, so now, I can relax, I am okay, and that is what matters. Well, there are several flaws in that theology. First, accepting Christ as our savior to forgive us our sins and to be redeemed is just as much about the here and now as the future. What Christ offers is purpose, the gifts of the Spirit to bring about the fruits of the Spirit in our lives, so that the world around us can see faith in Christ lived out, not so we get an out-of-hell free card, but a depth of life abundant that draws people to Christ. The world should be able to tell we are Christians by our love, our attitudes of grace and forgiveness, and the truth we live out. This aside, God convicts us of the need to be involved in the world, to reach the lost and make sure every soul has the opportunity to know Christ.

In our country, there is a church on most city blocks, and if the body of Christ is getting outside their walls, we should be changing the landscape of our country. In countries which are 99 percent Muslim or Buddhist or Hindu, they do not have those same opportunities, and if we can support missionaries or local pastors to be able to share in these places, we should be investing our time and talents to help.

That includes praying for the persecuted church around the world. There are places we literally cannot go, but we can be informed and invested in prayer and intercession. There are organizations which are able to step in and be the hands and feet of Christ in war-torn parts of the world. The point is, we have to be engaged, and it does not have to be either or. If we live here, we should be investing our lives into the people around us, but we can also pray and support organizations and individuals who God has called into those difficult places. We also need to be prepared to live lives obedient to whatever and wherever God calls us. When we get too comfortable, we stop listening.

We need to choose to be strategic. Now I will tell you that I have not planned a vacation for just the sake of vacation, I don't think ever. There have been some trips which were for work that we added a few days and made a mini-vacation too. We have planned trips to see family because building relationships and memories are important to us. Most of my adult trips have been because of missions. When the opportunity arises to go and pray for a people group or a country, it is my privilege and calling to do so. My question is, if we are living intentionally, can we not multitask and accomplish multiple things at the same time? What if we, living out our Christian faith, took vacations as a way to serve God? What if our destinations were places we purposely researched and prayed for, before we went, to find out opportunities or ways to connect while we are there and, at the same time, get away from routine?

Breaking out of routine is what Christian camps and retreats are all about, they give us a chance to reconnect with fellow believers and with God. So, what if every city we visit we pray for God to be revealed in new ways to those we are walking amid? What if we took notice of the needs around us and intentionally stepped in to bless others as we went along the way. What would that do for our families? What would that teach our children about priorities? What if the world saw Christians, who are Americans, going out of their way to be polite and bless others, to be servants rather than those expecting to be served? This does not cost us anything, but processing and seeking ways to live out the mandate to reach a lost world should be how we live every day. Even on our days off.

If you want to be renewed, energized, and filled, being self-absorbed will fail you, but if you are kingdom-absorbed, you will find energy beyond yourself to accomplish things you would never believe possible on your own power. That is just it, it is not about our power, it is Christ's power through us. When we get to the end of ourselves or step out of the way, that is when it becomes . . . watch out world! Watch what the living God can do!

I believe that in an age of automatic everything, getting people to slow down and notice the things of God will become even more difficult. I believe that is why there will be an outpouring of the

Spirit's power. I believe it is coming now, and I believe it is to reveal God in miraculous ways in a culture that has become so hardened. It will take this power to shake this world out of the trance that satan has lulled so many into and to break the web he has been weaving around us.

What gives me this hope when you turn on the news and see what appears to be a world spiraling down lower and lower? It is because He is alive in me. He is revealing Himself and His heart. He is using me in ways I could never have imagined nor I can fully comprehend; but that is okay, because it is not about me, it is about the God I serve. He is also using people I know and love, and I hear stories from around the world about how God is moving, but you won't find those stories on the news or in the headlines.

Chapter Eleven

Revisiting an All Too Familiar Season

When I hear people say that they are too busy to be involved, I will admit it frustrates me, because our availability has everything to do about our perspective and our priorities. We are accountable to God, and I myself have areas I need to continue to work on, not all my time is used as wisely as I should use it.

In about 2001 or so, I received a brochure about a new transitional Doctor of Physical Therapy degree. It came in the mail, and as I was looking at it, Eric came up behind me and said, "You need to do that." My response was "Are you crazy, I have too many responsibilities to do that." Well it was true I was running the rehabilitation department at the hospital in which I still saw a full load of patients, did the administrative work, and was a mother of four children, five if you counted Eric. We had horses, acres to mow, Sunday school to teach, sporting events to go to, friends we were still trying to help, getting up at three o'clock almost every morning to pray for whoever the Lord put in my heart. Could I really see me going back to college in the midst of my very busy and hectic life? Even I was not that crazy.

Eric said, "I know you, and you need to do this for you. If it means the rest of us stepping up to do more, so be it. You have carried more than your share; it is time we helped you." Have I mentioned that I love that man? He was serious, and he did know me. Still, doing something like this, just for me, didn't seem right.

There was talk about being a direct access state, where we would be initial contact for patients, and we would need to be good at differentiating whether an injury or pain was something safe for us to treat or if the patient should see their doctor first to rule out something not treatable with therapy. As the director, I was the go to person for questions and to help make suggestions for my staff, so this added education would really be a blessing for the hospital along with me.

At that point, I was wise enough to know that if God was not the one leading it, I wanted no part of it; so, I needed God to confirm that this was the right choice. As a result, I put out some fleeces, the first was getting my parents' blessing: their normal response would be to tell me kindly that I was being irresponsible and I should keep my focus on all I already had going on. So, when I told them, I had myself prepared for their answer, and they said exactly the opposite of what I expected. They said it was about time I do something for me, and that it was a chance for them and my family to help out more. Wow! I Did not see that coming. Then fleece two: I spoke to my director and human resources at the hospital. They were completely behind me, thought it made great sense for the department and they would help pay for it. Wow! Still not being convinced, I prayed again and told the Lord, I was willing to put in the work, but it really could not be about me, it had to be about Him and His will. I drove to work that morning, and would you like to guess what was there waiting on me? A rainbow. One placed directly over my off-site department.

Okay, Lord. So, I applied, was accepted, and returned to college life. Well, kind of. Based on the plan, it would take me 3-4 years to complete my degree. The program was built around working professionals. So each class was a combination of independent study, projects, a very long, long weekend, with ten- to twelve-hour days, a test and/or project at the end. You really could not take more than two classes at a time, and at times, I could only manage one, based on what season we were in with the kids. I quickly remembered why I could not be a professional student. Learning I love, tests and studying I could do without, and it had been more than fifteen years since being in college.

Well, for the class weekends, I would have to travel to college and they were an intense time, but it was also alone time with God. We would have some great conversations, and usually, I would come home refreshed spiritually and exhausted mentally and physically.

On one of my weekends at school, I had a crazy dream. It was so realistic it was scary. In the dream, I was in labor and gave birth to a beautiful baby girl, with lots of dark hair, just like my other two daughters. As I awoke, I told the Lord, "Man, that seemed real!" And I heard, "And you will name her Grace Elizabeth." I was in shock. I recognized His voice, but He was talking crazy talk. We had four wonderful children, ranging from six to fourteen. Having another baby was not in my plans at all, I was already thirty-seven and very happy with the family I was blessed with. Of course, I prayed and asked the Lord, "Are you serious?"

He was just giving me a heads up; so in a few months when I found out I was pregnant, I didn't have a heart attack. Even in this, I wanted His will not mine. I continued working, carrying a baby, and going to school.

As if I was bored, during this time, the Lord gave me a passion for the Jewish faith, and I studied the Old Testament, Jewish traditions, and tried to teach myself Hebrew. (I ultimately failed at accomplishing this task but enjoyed studying the letters and trying.) Gaining more insight into God's heart for the Jewish people was a part of my journey and the purpose of this season. I found some amazing Christian music sung in Hebrew, I still listen to it, and the sound of the shofar reaches the depths of me. I am sure this does not come as a surprise to you, but God has a heart and is seeking to bring unto Himself, through Jesus, the Jewish people.

Well, I did give birth to a beautiful healthy baby girl in January of 2002. It was our year to host Eric's family for Christmas, and we had waited until the first of January to maximize those who could attend. I was eight and a half months pregnant, and even though I love entertaining, it was a bit much for me, mainly because the way

God wired me, I can never do things halfway and wanted everything to look inviting and festive, and I wanted a fancy dinner. So, by the time all of his siblings and their families arrived, I was exhausted. I was thrilled to have them there, but exhausted.

As if that was not enough, Eric's youngest brother and his family were the last to arrive, because they had just had a horrible flu sweep through their family and Jon had caught the tail end of it, and this was his first time venturing out. His wife said they were exposed to it at her family gathering, and within a few hours, kids started getting sick and dropping like flies.

My first thought was, that is impossible, no one gets a flu that quickly, many viruses take ten to fifteen days to incubate and cause symptoms; but anyway, I sure hope that they are not contagious still. One thing which is more miserable than being almost nine months pregnant is puking when you are that big and uncomfortable. We had a lovely time and meal. I had fixed grownup food (turkey mignons) and had shaved ham and roast beef for kids who did not want anything requiring a knife. We laughed, opened presents, and then everyone headed home, which was two to four hours for everyone.

About an hour after everyone left, we started getting calls, everyone was stopping by the side of the road because of all the vomiting. My first thought was, did I feed them something bad causing food poisoning? When we started tracking what everyone ate, there was not one common thing between those sick.

Then it hit us. It was the worst, most virulent flu I have ever seen. My sister-in-law called it the attic flu. Whatever you wanted to name it, it was horrible. Everyone was lying on the floor, in a bathroom moaning. My family will tell you that I can handle debriding infected wounds, burns, and gangrene, but keep me away from puke. I felt a little nauseated, but that could have been a result of hearing five people vomiting almost simultaneously. Music is great in stereo, puking not so much.

Instead of having the same symptoms everyone else had, I started shaking. I was shaking so violently all over that I could not hold a glass and get it to my mouth to drink from it. It got so bad that we went to the ER. The doctor who saw me was convinced that

I was just scared about having a baby. Right! This is pregnancy number six and I am just now going to get so freaked out I am going to shake myself into labor. Well, he was NO help. As I prayed about it, I realized that the virus had attacked everyone else's GI tract but my nervous system.

You cannot really do anything but treat the symptoms of a virus and wait it out. Well, I ended up in labor a couple of days later, and they were taking her C-section. When we got back to the room and they brought her in the bassinet, I realized she was shaking too. It did not last long for her, but it literally took me over six months to stop shaking completely. If I got overtired or stressed, I would start shaking. The drive home from the hospital was the first time in my life I experienced an anxiety attack and claustrophobia. The blessing is I can sympathize in a deeper way when someone struggles with those things now.

Truly I believe, that is part of the way God uses what is intended for harm to turn it into blessing. If the purpose of our lives is to be in relationship with God and others, everything which helps us connect on a deeper level is actually a blessing. Some would say, how can a loving God allow tragedies to happen? They miss the point, that God allows humans free will and there is sin in the world, impacting lives on all levels. God is merciful and loving. There are many times when I sense a heaviness and will have tears just flow, and when I pray about it, something has grieved the heart of God, and the Holy Spirit wants me to understand that.

As a mother, I speak truth to my children. Sometimes they listen sometimes they choose to ignore my advice, they still make their own decisions. Some of them bring heartache, that is when I come alongside and hold them, encourage them, and try to help them move forward wiser for the experience. Of course, God does the same thing, doesn't He? It would take a lot of nerve for my kids to blame me for what happens in their lives, but for some reason, we want to do that to God. Now disease and death are a result of the fall, human choice. If we had listened to God then, we would not be in the place we are now. There would be no disease, death, or decay. Now we have to complete our journey here to be able to return to the life God truly desires for us. When someone takes the shortcut and something or someone steals them away from this life, we see this as tragedy, but is it? Our perspective is so limited.

Well, back to the story. Having Grace was and is such a blessing. God's plan is so much better than mine; He has shown me that over and over. Having a baby and recovering from my illness slowed my progress with my degree, but I was able to get back on track. It was challenging having a baby, nursing her, working and studying, and still being engaged in the lives of my four other children, my husband, and to find time for God. Well, I was absolutely at the end of me and depending on God to make it all work, and He did. You know He never fails to live up to your expectations. If you expect nothing, you see nothing; if you expect everything, He is in everything and you see it. One of the greatest gifts is to be given clear vision, to see God in everything. He is in His creation, working in and through people and the interactions around you.

At year four of my degree plan, I was almost a year behind where I had originally planned, but I was just blessed with the surprise of bonus child two, double bonus if you would. Her name was Hope Victoria. She was unexpected, but she was such a ray of sunshine. She was blessed with such a loving spirit, and I have watched her bless so many.

We would take the little girls with us to see some of the elderly people God has put in our lives, and Hope would love on them with a way that was awe-inspiring. God does not make mistakes, and when you live a life surrendered to Him, He will not let it get boring either! Austin was the only senior graduating from high school with a two-month old sister and a mother still in college. Adventure, I warned you.

Year five brought the completion of my degree. Praise the Lord! What was I going to do with all my free time? Well, God had plans. Eric and I had looked forward to eventually going to the mission field on short-term trips and potentially a long-term placement once the kids were grown. Well, bonus children five and six were going to leave us retirement age by the time we had all the kids grown and through college, so God worked out another option.

Chapter Twelve

Flame

It is interesting what God will bring into our path to be a catalyst for transition. One of the things which rekindled the flame to get us involved with missions was our taking "The Perspectives" course. It served as a resetting for our vision for a world in need of the gospel.

This course was also a part of what had precipitated the changes for missions in our church. We were strategically changing the paradigm of how we do missions, a work that is still being fleshed out even now. We want partnerships. The days of the American church seeming like the white knight to save the world with their money and their way of doing things may have been well-intentioned, but over time, we have discovered in some ways it did not work all that well. There are some great books that highlight some of the failures of our throwing money at things without truly knowing the people, their needs, and their struggles. You hear of well-intentioned Christians who have built churches and houses and sent equipment like tractors only to return years later and find nature reclaiming them, and when asked, the people say, "You never came back to fix your building," or "We had no one who could repair the tractor."

We need to look at what the ramifications of our actions are to the local economies. Are we putting national people out of work when we go in and build homes or provide shoes or do dental work or any number of other activities we have been known to invest in.

Can we find a way to use gifts and talents or expertise partnering with local businesses or individuals to help move them forward in sustainable work for them in the future while moving God's kingdom forward?

The parable of giving a man a fish today, he will be hungry tomorrow, but if we teach him how to fish he can feed himself and teach others to do the same. This is the direction we wanted to go. Instead of making our brothers and sisters in Christ around the world dependent on us and our resources, we teach them to look at their own resources and develop a plausible strategy and plan, and help them implement those plans and strategies and at the same time allowing them to teach us about how they have seen God show up. The depth of the body of Christ in areas where there is persecution is deep. They have figured out ways to work around hardship and have witnessed the work of the Holy Spirit in miraculous ways on almost a daily frequency; they have insights and wisdom that we need.

Once things settled a little, opportunities to do some short-term mission trips came up on the horizon. In the spring of 2009, our church wanted to assess a missionary couple for possible partnering with. At the same time, an organization we support was planning to take a prayer team to this same location for potential training and partnering with them also. The organization was expecting to make a second leg of the trip, which was not connected to our church, and I was invited to continue on it if I wanted. Both parts were prayer trips in which we were called to be praying for insight and wisdom on next steps in these places and for spiritual breakthrough.

They thought it might be to Africa, and when I heard that, I remembered the dream with the African warriors and another dream I had about an African refugee camp, which I had been awakened to intercede for. If the second leg of the trip was to Africa, I would not hesitate.

It was a little disappointing when I was told the second leg of the trip would be to the Philippines. That was not such an obvious decision, so I spent some time in prayer about whether God was calling me to go there. Finally, a couple of weeks later, I notified them I would go to the Philippines.

That very night, I experienced something like I would see in a scary movie, if I watched scary movies. I was sound asleep when I was startled awake by the sensation I was being strangled and unable to breathe. I tried to nudge Eric to awaken him to no avail, and not being able to speak, I hit him in the side. He startled awake and sat up. He looked at me and said he thought I was under spiritual attack. I nodded but was still unable to speak. We both dropped to our knees and began praying for release. It quickly stopped, and I could breathe and speak.

It was disturbing to be awoken so violently, but we both tried to lie back down to try to sleep the remainder of the night, but it was not meant to be. Grace came into the bedroom very upset. She was crying, and between the sobs, I made out that she was awoken by a voice which told her that if her mommy went on this trip she would die. Grace was seven at the time, and we were up the rest of the night wrestling, not physically but spiritually. The voice she heard was the enemy, but I did not want to scare her more. As I held her and tried to get her to stop crying, she would say, "If you love me you won't go, right?" And I told her I was called to go and I had to be obedient to God above all else. She would cry and say, "Then you promise to come home?" And I would tell her I could not promise something I did not have control over. I would tell her that only God knew the numbers of my days and that if it was my time to go, it would not matter if I was at home in bed, walking down the street, or on the other side of the world. Then we would start over with, "Don't you love us? If you loved us, you wouldn't leave us." It was the longest most exhausting night of my life, and that is saying something!

As we made preparations for the trip, I had a peace about it. I trusted God and His sovereignty. It was also clear that the enemy did not want me to go on it, which was confirmation in my mind that I absolutely needed to go. As I sat in the plane in Dayton, I opened my Bible to Joshua 1, where God tells Joshua to claim everyplace his feet tread as part of the Promised Land. I sensed my assignment began with claiming everywhere I stepped for Christ.

Then I looked at our itinerary and remembered this flight was landing in Washington, D.C., and that seemed like a great place to start claiming for Christ. As I thought about my assignment and prayed, I just felt like it would be so much better if I was able to step on the ground rather than the floor of the airport; but I was not sure how to make it happen, I resigned myself to the fact that the foundation of the airport sits on the ground. As we got closer to DC, the leader of our trip mentioned that we might try to go out into DC as we had a few hours layover. Then, as we got closer, he said, on second thought, to leave the international airport terminal and to get back through security, even three hours might not be enough, so we would just sit in the airport. My hopes were lifted and dashed within minutes. As we were landing, they came on the intercom and said that they had been redirected and we would not be able to get to the gate directly, we would have to depart from the plane and walk to the gate door. I smiled.

As I stepped down onto the pavement, I began praying. The funny thing was the leader looked at me and said, "You have an assignment, don't you!" I acknowledged that I did. The woman right behind me with our group left her passport on the plane and she had to run back and get it, so I was able to linger longer while waiting for her. I claimed our nation's capital for God in the precious name of Jesus Christ. I also thanked God for making a way when it didn't seem there was one. He is great at that; it is one of His specialties!

Once we got in the airport and at our gate, we had some questions. And when we went up to the airline desk, the woman behind it was, well, curt; actually kind of nasty and grumpy all at the same time. She was German, and she had that no-nonsense way about her. Well, after we had all been put in our place by her, we had another question, and I got voted to go up and ask; they said I had a way with people. Haha! What they meant to say is we don't want to do this, and you look gullible.

Well, I just chuckled and marched up to the desk. She was looking down, that kind of "I know you are there, but if I look busy maybe you will go away" thing. Well, I didn't, and she finally acknowledged me. In her curt tone, she said, "Was it your goal today to just irritate me?" Well, being the people-person I am, I just played along and responded with, "Yep, I woke up this morning and said to myself, I want to make sure I really irritate the stewardess on my flight to Frankfurt. How am I doing?" Well, my response caught her off guard, and she smiled. I got my answer and marched back to the row of fellow travelers, who were all sitting with their mouths open.

Victory on both fronts, I thought to myself. They asked, "How did you do that? You actually got her to smile." I just smiled an ornery little smile. Well, I am an observer, particularly an observer of people, and I observed a woman who was stressed and unhappy. She found no joy in life. So I decided since I had a couple of hours to spare, I would look for a flower to present to this woman, to brighten her gloomy, sad day. Well, I looked high and low and could not find a flower in the airport, and time was drawing short. So, I looked around for something which would not cost an arm and a leg and would brighten her day. Well, my eyes landed on a pinwheel, with the design of stars and stripes of the American flag; that will do, I thought.

Well, I marched back up to the podium she was standing behind, and I kept my little gift down low where she would not see it. Since she continued to look busy and unapproachable, she did not see me coming. When she looked up, she said in a little less irritated tone than previously, "Well, what do you want now?" I smiled and held up her pinwheel, and I handed it to her. She was shocked, but reached out and took it, and I said "Have a great day and God bless you." Then I turned and walked away. Shortly after that interaction, I sat and prayed. I prayed for her and sensed this had been a divine appointment. Something significant happened in the spiritual realm with this small gesture of kindness toward a stranger. I believe it had to do with a softening between a German and an American, as if a stronghold had been broken.

The airline then changed our gate, and we were ushered to a much bigger and busier area. As I sat and people watched, I felt someone softly touch my shoulder. When I turned, it was the German stewardess. She told me that I had made her day, the ray of sunshine she needed. Thank you, Lord, for helping me sense and hear what is not spoken. Well, our flight across to Frankfurt was very long, and I was trapped in the middle of the row. There were two people to the right and the lady to my left had placed her luggage under her feet and had her legs up high on the back of the seat in front of her; somehow, she was able to sleep.

I sat there for eleven hours. I would doze off, but not for long. I did fall deep enough asleep during that time to have two dreams. The first was of multiple small groups of people just going through the motions: one was a couple putting a cup down on a coffee table, someone else was working a sewing machine. Then I realized that one of the groups included my friend Dr. Mirza, who had passed away while on a trip to bring his mother home from Pakistan to the United States. I tripped on the corner of the coffee table spilling the cup of liquid. All of a sudden, my act of clumsiness had broken everyone out of their trances, and Dr. Mirza saw me and asked why I had not helped him see, and he challenged me that it was not too late for others. Well, a great sadness came over me even in my dream, as I knew he died a Muslim man without Christ. He put the challenge forth to help others see Christ, even at the expense of my pride. Was I willing to make a fool of myself to help the lost see? Yes, I am willing.

The next dream was gross. I was standing in this big parking lot, and it was covered with worms and maggots, and I could feel them crunching under my feet. I was on tiptoes trying to get out of there while I was cringing and saying, "Ew, ew . . . this is so gross." I awoke to the phrase, "You will trample death every step that you take." Well, what is up with that? I wondered what Lord means by that. I prayed about it but tried not to dwell on it.

We landed in Delhi, India, and took a taxi to a YWCA to spend the night. There were three women on the trip at that point, and the other two did not want to be alone. In my world, "alone" is a luxury. Not to say I would want to always be alone, but I can pray more intently. With six kids, alone just doesn't happen very often.

The room was fine; nothing fancy, but clean. There were high windows, with no glass, so I laid there in the dark and listened to an Indian man chant all night. I had no idea what he was saying, but I laid there and prayed for him and his soul. I prayed for this country and the people, so many lost but beautiful people. There is a smell to India, especially the big cities; I believe it comes from the burning cow dung they use to heat their water and their chai and to cook over.

As I laid and prayed, I noticed how heightened all my senses were. They were occupied with the sights I had already seen and the sounds and smells of this place. I was not in Kansas or Indiana anymore.

We awoke, grabbed a bite to eat, and loaded in a car heading to the airport to take a domestic flight to Dehradun. The problem was, I had a nasty headache; it felt like a tight band around my head, and the pressure was very strong. I became nauseated, and while we were waiting everyone else ate chicken at McDonald's in the airport, I was feeling too ill to eat.

We boarded the plane, and of course, it was small compared to the other planes on the trip. They had us seated, and you could smell the spicy food on board, and I knew I was in trouble. I rushed to the bathroom, but the stewardess put her hand on the door and asked me to sit back down. Well, let's just say she regretted stopping me. We got the mess cleaned up, and I sat in my seat, just praying for God to help me. I felt terrible, and we had not even been here a half a day yet.

We landed in Dehradun and it was 120 degrees. The group wanted us to stop for supper, and they went to an air-conditioned restaurant. They had me go in with them, thinking that cooling me off would help, but the smell was too much again.

I went out and sat in the heat in the back of the car. I had the window down a few inches hoping for some airflow. I closed my eyes to pray when a little boy came up and tried to reach in; he wanted money. We had been warned not to give anyone money, as it will bring a mob running. But it was torture to have to listen to this boy the entire time the group ate in the restaurant. The band around my head persisted, and I felt so ill, I could not even pray.

The leader came out to check on me, and I told him about not even being able to pray at that point, so he prayed over me. That gave enough relief that I could now pray. I noticed that this distinct band persisted, as though I had a physical band around my head. I asked who the men were that had the tight turbans on their heads, and he said they were Sikhs. Then it came to me, I asked, "What was the temple we were next to at the YWCA?" He said it was a Sikh temple. That was the source of my headache and illness, so I prayed once again for the Sikh man and sent my love and forgiveness to him, in the precious name of Jesus, for putting a curse on me. Immediately, the band was broken and the headache subsided. The leader chuckled and said, "So you are the lightning rod." Great! That sounded like fun, not.

Once we wound our way up the mountainside on these steep grades and hairpin turns, we arrived at our destination in Uttarakhand, India. We were taken to the inn and went to our rooms to go to bed, in what seemed to be a cross between a hotel and a bed-and-breakfast. Tomorrow would be another day.

We awoke to no water available in the building. The host arrived to find out how our night went, and he was very upset to hear we had no water. He interpreted the situation as though the inn was not nice enough. He kept apologizing, we assured him that it was fine but would be helpful to have water. He decided that there was a nicer hotel, and he left to make arrangements. It saddened us all to have given the impression we needed nicer.

We then gathered for prayer. There was a designated prayer leader from the organization we were travelling with, and he asked if anyone felt God was leading them or the group a specific direction. The Lord had given me a vision, but knowing how some people need to have a little time to warm up and feel comfortable sharing, I always hesitate to jump right in, as I don't want to shut anyone down, and some people need to have the discomfort of silence to step out of their comfort zone. Well, no one responded, so I raised my hand and said as I was praying during the night the Lord had given me a vision.

The vision I had was vivid and detailed and kind of a video clip, if you will, as there was some movement. It was of a woman, bound in grave clothes, standing on the hillside, right at one of the hairpin turns. All I could see from a distance was that the only thing exposed was her face; otherwise, she was covered from head to toe. She had black hair, and just the edge of her hair was visible at her forehead. There was a sorrowful look, and she was crying out for help; she was trapped. As I thought of the vision, it altered to a second perspective, with the woman, still bound in grave clothes, but now seeing layers around her like a babushka nesting doll from Russia. My spirit sensed that this woman, whoever she was, she was key to this place and she needed to be set free.

Well, I was shocked when the prayer leader looked right at me and said, "God forewarned me that someone would sidetrack us, and there are all kinds of women around the world in bondage, we are going to disregard this vision." Truthfully, I was a little embarrassed, but I also understand authority, and he was put in authority on this prayer journey, and I deflected to his authority. The thing is, that vision never left, and to this day, it remains unchanged. It was one of my failures.

During this trip, we did a lot of hiking up and down the mountainside, and after that first day, I began having an ache in my left knee. This was unusual, as I had never really had knee pain previously; but I don't climb the Himalayas everyday either, and some of the trails and paths were rocky and uneven, so I dismissed it as having torqued it a bit.

As we finished on our first day, they took us to the other hotel, and we were on the second floor. As I climbed the steps, I became very short of breath, so as soon as I got to my room, I used my inhaler. Thankfully, I had been warned by a friend who had been to this place previously, he had not had issues with his asthma in years, but it became an issue for him here; therefore, I came prepared with an inhaler.

I was again alone in my room. The first night in this new hotel was very difficult. My chest felt like it was on fire, and it just pained and burned all night long. There was no sleeping through it. I just lay in my bed and cried and prayed. I reminded God, like He needed a reminder, that I was here to serve Him and be obedient, and I needed Him; I could not do it without Him, so I needed Him to hold me through whatever was going on. When I got up the next morning and the knee felt swollen and stiff, especially in the back, it clicked. I had a blood clot in my leg, and it had broken off and gone to my lungs. We gathered to pray and go on about our day. I told the team what my concerns were, and they just nodded and prayed for me. I could tell they had no idea that this was a life-threatening situation, and we still had about a week here before we headed to the Philippines.

The thing is, I weighed my options. If I went to a clinic or hospital, the trip was over for me. Eric, my kids, my parents, none of them had passports, so I would be on my own in India. My other option was to keep persevering and trust God. My spirit knew I was supposed to be on this trip, and I did not want to give this win to the enemy.

We walked and prayed over spiritually significant places and went into some unreached areas. Not as deep, by any means, as the missionaries there, who would walk up into the mountains for days to reach people. Normally, I am a very fast walker, but now I walked much slower, and there were times we would walk part way up and I would have to stop and pray alone, because I could not physically go any further due to the pains in my chest and knee. God was faithful, and I remember one spot in particular where I really sensed the Lord's presence, and I was able to pray and cry out to the Lord for the lost souls in this part of the world, begging Him to set them free from those things which hindered their hearing the truth and coming to Him. Rarely do you get to hear if these types of prayer trips have an impact, but it was this very place that another group from our church came only a few weeks later. The group, including several of our youth, met a demon-possessed woman on the same path. The group came around her and prayed for her release. Now this was way outside the box for our group, but they saw God work in a way they had never seen before, and their faith grew as a result.

As I stood on the side of this mountain, I could look down into the valley. With a mist rising up, it was breathtaking, and I had the privilege to be there. God is amazing. God has a heart for the Hindus who worship idols and make futile offerings, leaving them lost and hopeless. Inviting evil to reside and control them.

There was one missionary couple who were instrumental to the ministry in this section of India, and I was able to hear the heart of the wife as I spent extra time with her. She was strikingly beautiful and very intelligent. She shared about the burden of her husband's passion and calling to reach far into the unreached areas, but of her loneliness and despair. She had been dealing with chronic pain, which would leave her unable to function. We prayed together and cried together.

There can be this strange clash that people find themselves a part of, changing roles and expectations due to modern technology and thoughts, but an obligation to cultural taboos and standards which are in direct conflict with the other. She was one of those women trapped between these two worlds. She was the woman in the vision. She is still trapped in grave clothes, now several years later. For me, it is a reminder that, personally, I have to follow God and not man. Now, that is not to say I should ignore authority, but I now see that in this situation, God had given me the authority, and I released it to someone who did not understand. I should have just quietly prayed and focused on the assignment He had given me. Remember, God always uses things which satan intends for harm for good. For these missionaries, that has not yet been revealed, but I trust Him. For me, it is part of the training ground, a refining process.

Once we left India, we headed to the Philippines. We started in Manila and met with a group of missionaries. A team which had been through the fire of spiritual battle, and there were casualties. The original two leaders, one died of a stroke, one of cancer; another one of the men had been attacked by an evil spirit causing such severe back pain he had to be medevacked to his home country, where, for three months, the doctors could not find any cause or offer any relief. His home church decided to fast and pray for him, and that broke the stronghold and stopped his back pain.

This team had worked twenty years on translating the Injil into the native language. The Injil is the Gospel of Jesus Christ, which is part of the Muslim holy books. This ministry was developing relationships to reach the Muslims in the southern part of the Philippines. We ended up in Zamboanga, a very hostile area to Americans and Christians.

We were taken to a secure place to stay, and we were not to leave our room. We travelled by vehicles with blacked-out windows to conceal our color. It was an interesting journey. We learned about their ministry, and we prayed around the city, not by foot this time but by car.

There was one place they felt held spiritual significance and we needed to go to and pray. It was a fort which was now a museum. It was on the coast overlooking the ocean. It was where many battles to lay claim on the Philippines had taken place by many different nations. As we entered, we were told not to draw attention to ourselves and to walk and pray with our eyes open. One of the leaders asked if anyone knew where we were to start.

Well, as soon as we entered, I knew my assignment, and I simply said, "I don't know about you guys, but I am supposed to start over there." Over there was one of the far corners from the entrance. But I planned on meandering over there alone; you know, not drawing any attention. Several in the group said they didn't know where to start, and so everyone followed me; so much for not-drawing-attention gang. As I got closer to the corner, there was a large white gate with CLOSED and No Entrance in red painted across it. Behind it was a rampart to the top of the fort.

Seeing that gate and sign, once I got partway there, I turned around and faced opposite the gate. I just needed to stand and pray in the area. I sensed that there had been much death in this area, and I wanted to seek guidance on how to pray. While I am standing and praying, eyes open, everyone else is talking among themselves. Then I hear someone say, "Oh no, don't look now but there is a guard heading right at us." Someone said something about looking nonchalant.

As I looked up, I realized he was heading straight toward me, and like the parting of the red sea, everyone else must have noticed that and stepped aside. He walked right up to me and said, "You want to go there?" Looking behind me, I said no, I saw the signs. He repeated again, less like a question and more like a direction. This time, I decided to say "Yes?" He motioned for me to follow him, and I did, so did everyone else. He unlocked and moved the gate aside, and he stayed right by me. It was the strangest thing; he never spoke or even acknowledged anyone else in the group.

As I walked up the rampart, I knew there had been so much loss in this area, loss of life, loss of freedom, loss of hope. I had to push back tears. When we got to the top, he looked me in the eyes and said, "This fort was built on the lives of the Filipino slaves." My eyes welled up with tears again, and all I could say was "that grieved God's heart, I am so sorry." While he and I spoke, everyone else looked out over the ocean and prayed. He told me how just past the fort, on the beach, homeless people had built lean-to homes and it ended up a little village, but the government did not want them there, so they burned them out, and many people had died there also.

He then asked me if I wanted to walk around the top of the fort, and being a quick study, I just said yes. He kicked some trash aside, and we walked around the top of the fort and prayed. This was not a tourist area, there was broken glass from light bulbs and debris to be stepped over. As we walked around, he shared about how the Dutch had tried to take over, the Spanish, and several others. We continued to pray for forgiveness, for the harm that was done, the arrogance and greed of man. When we got back in the vehicle, someone said, "What just happened in there?" Only God knows for sure, but this was part of the reason I was called to this leg of the trip. We laughed and wondered if we had just been given a tour by an angel, it seemed so surreal. One thing I will repeat, we serve an amazing God, who cares about all people. He was seeking healing and softening my heart for those oppressed and the Muslims.

Well, I have not mentioned my health at this point, but I had continued to struggle, and the swelling in my leg continued to increase. The first few days in Manila, we were staying in the missionary's home with food I could eat. It was helping me feel better, even though the pains in my knee and chest continued. I had spoken to the leader and told him I really needed some aspirin before the flight home, and he had shared a couple of his small supply throughout the week. He kindly went walking and found a pharmacy open late and purchased some aspirin for me to take on the flight home.

As soon as I landed in Detroit, I called my husband and told him I was in trouble, and since it was Saturday (now thirty-six hours into Saturday I believe) he needed to contact our doctor and find out what to do, as waiting to see him Monday did not seem smart. Our doctor was also a friend, and Eric called back in just a couple minutes and said he did not want me to go home, but rather directly to the hospital. All six of my children were home and were coming to the airport to pick me up, so I told Eric to tell them I would go to the ER after dinner with my family. The little girls would need to see me before I was put in the hospital.

When I got to Fort Wayne, we went to dinner, and then Eric took me to the hospital. The ER doctor had lived as a missionary exactly where I had been in India. It is such a small world. They did lab work and a CT scan and admitted me. My doctor came in and said he couldn't believe I stopped to have dinner when I developed this clot on the flight home. I laughed and said, it developed on the flight over. He literally fell backward and hit the wall as he said, "How are you alive? You should not be here." Then he said, "This is a miracle!" I had no iron in my blood, he did not know you could be alive with no iron. I was two pints low on blood. I had multiple pulmonary emboli (over forty) and any one of them could have taken my life. I had hiked up mountain and hillsides, taken six flights after it started. Do you remember the dream and what God told me when I awoke from it? "You will trample death every step that you take." It was literal. That evil presence which tried to choke me and told Grace I would die if I went on this trip had tried multiple times, but God held me back from the grip of death over and over and over. He had asked me to claim for Him and His kingdom every place I tread on this trip. Once I got home and was praying about it, I realized I had travelled all the way around the world, touching down in DC, Frankfurt, Delhi, Dehradun, Kuala Lumpur, Tokyo, and Detroit. The enemy did not want me making it all the way. Now do I fully understand all of it, no way! My mind could not fully comprehend the plans of God or what actually happens in the spiritual realm when a life is fought over or when we claim for Christ what had been stolen or when we reach out to bless a stranger. Even though I don't get it all, I do get that God wants us to be a part of something much bigger than ourselves, a part of what He is doing. What a privilege it is to serve God, and how humbling to know that the Creator of the universe is calling His people. He is calling you. Will you answer the call?

Chapter Thirteen

Opportunities Here, There, and Everywhere

My next international adventure occurred in my small hometown. Now if that does not make much sense, you can understand my surprise. We were just headed on a walk with the little girls to get ice-cream downtown. We had just stepped onto the sidewalk in front of our house when Eric got a call that his dad had taken a turn for the worse, and he needed to head to Texas. He grabbed a backpack with a change of clothes and headed to Texas. The girls were disappointed that Dad had left and that they did not get their ice-cream.

So we headed out the door again to get some ice-cream, a three-block walk. We had to cross one very busy street which goes through town. As we crossed this busy street, a half a block from home, we saw an unusual site. There, standing on the corner, were four very small women, who had an oriental look. They looked lost and confused. As has been identified previously, my hometown's ethnic diversity is very limited.

Stopping to see if we could help, we quickly discovered that they did not speak English well. Their vocabulary was very limited, about four or five words. They used gestures and a few words to explain. They were Chinese—no Chinese pulling, their eyes slanted, and they made walking motion with their fingers; "taxi" and "shop" were the words I could make out and with gestures. What I gathered was that they were looking for a taxi to take them shopping. Well, they would have stood on that corner a very long time, as there is not a taxi in Wabash. I tried to explain to them the only place to shop after six would be Wal-Mart. They understood that and wanted directions on how to walk there. Well, that was not wise; there were not sidewalks the whole way, and there would be four lanes of traffic to cross over to get to Wal-Mart, and it would be getting dark by the time they were done.

So, I did what any crazy person would do. I offered to drive them to Wal-Mart. My gestures and sign language were understood, so we walked back the half block to the parked van. I drove them to Wal-Mart, and they said thanks and gestured they would walk back. I shook my head no and pointed to one of their watches and asked when to come back to pick them up. They pointed at the number ten. That would give them over three hours of shopping in Wal-Mart. The two youngest girls would be in bed by then, and Faith would be home from work.

When I arrived to pick them up, they were not outside, so I went in to discover that they all four were still shopping. One had a cart of vitamins and minerals; one had half a cart of room deodorizers. This was one very interesting shopping excursion. We rounded them up and went to the checkout. One of the ladies, Rena, was not getting her card to work. So, I paid for her purchase.

Then there was Gunar, she called her daughter in college in California. She wanted me to speak with her. Her daughter became the interpreter. She wanted me to know how much the ladies appreciated my kindness in taking them to the store. She explained that they were travelling with a musical group and they were from a portion of China, which was called Urumqi. They do not consider themselves Chinese, hence the Chinese–no Chinese from my first meeting. I did find out that they were staying at the downtown hotel and would be performing the next night. When I got them back to their hotel, they asked me to go up with them; they wanted me to speak to Gunar's daughter again. Well, it was quite comical; they wanted to know my beauty secrets, which made me look so young. I had to laugh out loud, but they were serious. Soap and water, I told them. They had seen advertisements about these youth serum products that the women of America use, so I gathered that Americans are not the only ones sucked in by advertising. They were greatly disappointed that I didn't have any beauty secrets to share. You would think one look at me and they could have figured that out. They gave me two beautiful silk scarves as a thank you. I tried to refuse, but you could tell they would have been offended. Gunar's daughter said that they came with them to give out as they travelled as expressions of thanks. While speaking to Gunar's daughter, I asked what they had planned for their Saturday. They had hoped to shop, but with the limited choices, they did not know. I offered to take them to Fort Wayne to shop, and when it was translated for them, they were ecstatic.

Faith and I picked them up. We had the little girls spend the day at Grandma's as there would not be enough room in the van for everyone. Driving and listening to the now five ladies speaking what I discovered was Uighur. They know Mandarin Chinese but do not like to use it. We had a lot of fun showing the ladies an outdoor shopping mall, which offered much more the selection they had hoped for.

The group they were travelling with was going across the country playing for schools and doing some local performances the next evening. They travelled by bus, so their opportunities to shop were limited. From what I understood, there are many things here much less expensive than there, even though many of the things come from China. They don't make things for their people to buy, they want Americans to buy them.

When we got back from shopping, I took them to dinner. When I bowed to say grace, they asked if I was Muslim. I said no, I was a follower of Jesus Christ. They smiled and nodded and gestured that they were all Muslim. We continued our miming and gesturing through dinner. When we got them to their hotel, they asked us to please come to their performance that evening.

So we did. It was beautiful. Rena was one of two cup dancers. She had a full cup and saucer she balanced on her head as the others played traditional music. The instruments were very interesting. I could see the ladies we knew looking around as they performed, I thought maybe trying to find us. There were men travelling in the group also. And when one of the men was doing a love ballad, he spotted Faith and came down to the audience and serenaded her. So then, the ladies knew we were there.

After the show was over, I went to the stage door and knocked, and the gentleman who answered said we could not enter; he must have been the manager of the trip. As soon as I mentioned Gunar's name, he smiled and said, "Oh, it is you, please come back." He hollered back and out came the ladies in their costumes. We visited and laughed at the difficulty in communication. They wanted pictures with us, and the men all went gaga over Faith; she was at least six to eight inches taller than the tallest man. They all wanted their picture with her. We exited to allow them to go see people in the lobby.

The crazy thing was that once they came out, they just hovered around us. When we departed, the ladies actually cried. They asked us to come visit them in their country anytime. They said that they would welcome us and show us their city, please would we come. It was ridiculous in human terms. We had known these ladies only a little more than twenty-four hours, and yet there was a bond, a closeness that was shared. They hugged and kissed each of us and thanked us again for our kindness and reiterated the invitation to come visit them. A divine appointment, absolutely a divine appointment. The ironic thing is, it would not have happened if Eric had not gotten the call to go to Texas or if he delayed until the next morning to head out. God uses all things, even tragedies, to orchestrate something beautiful in the midst of where we are.

My spirit sensed that there was more to this interaction than what we could see. It was confirmed when we went to dinner with friends, one who travels to unreached people groups to teach business as missions. When I told them the crazy story, he asked if these people were Weegers. "Why yes, I believe that is what the program called them." I responded. He laughed out loud and said, "Only you . . . the Weegers are a very closed Muslim culture found in China, and there have been people trying to reach them for years and cannot get in, and here you are in Wabash with an open invitation to go."

OPPORTUNITIES HERE, THERE, AND EVERYWHERE

Now if the Lord provides the opportunity, I would love to go, and so would Faith. Somehow, even if I don't go, I believe the relationships and invitations given with such heartfelt enthusiasm have broken through some of the cultural and spiritual barriers to that region. It is my prayer that God will continue building relationships of friendship and trust to provide the opportunity to speak the truth of Jesus Christ into the lives of a proud and oppressed people group in China, but not Chinese.

This is an example how God can use us if we stay observant or open to altering our schedules. So many times in our daily routine, we don't take the time to notice people and situations around us because we have our own goals and plans for the day. If we will just take the time to slow down and be open to what God may have for us, right where we are, you never know what adventure might be standing across the street. God wants to use us here, there, and everywhere.

Chapter Fourteen

India the Least of These

The next mission trip outside the country occurred three months later. It was a discerning-prayer trip on the front end and a community assessment planning and business as missions training on the back end. We were trying to decide which areas we would be able to build the best two-way relationships, while at the same time reaching into some unreached areas. We also were underwriting training in Uganda, which was funded with money raised by a "Radical auction," after one of the adult Sunday school classes had read David Platt's book *Radical*.

Just a month or so before our next trip, one of the Indian pastors we wanted to get to know more was in the USA for fund-raising through their supporting denomination. They wanted to meet us, and they flew to Indiana for a day or two. As we drove down to pick up this couple, I was praying. I was sitting in the back by myself, so I did not have to be involved in the conversation up front the whole time. I was thanking God for this opportunity to meet this pastor and his wife. Then I heard the Lord say, "Do you trust me?" As I mentioned before, I hear that at times, and it is usually to prepare me for something God wants me to step into. So I assured Him I did trust Him. He continued to ask, and my answer remained yes. You start to feel like Peter must have when Jesus asked him three times if he loved Him. Then the Lord told me He was going to take me into the dark places, and I would be His light, but I needed to trust

Him. He would be with me, was I willing? He is such a gentleman, He always asks, even though I have told Him more times than I can count or remember that my life is His to use. It is my heart's desire to be used by Him to be a blessing to others, to help set the captives free, and for that to bless Him.

As I prayed and went deeper into what God wanted to prepare me for, I realized we were at the Indianapolis airport already to pick up our passengers. We found them and had a good conversation on the way back to Wabash. As we drew closer to our church, we got quiet and prayed together, seeking God's blessing and discernment for this Indian pastor and his wife and our pending trip.

As we were praying out loud, I verbalized and confirmed my willingness to be available and to be used and sensed excitement for the opportunity that God was going to provide. As we pulled up to the church, there was a rainbow positioned right over the building. One of the men commented, "Hey look, there is a rainbow." And he looked at me and said, "I believe that is meant for you." I chuckled and said, "Yes, I believe it is." Now, the funny thing is I had never told anyone in that van about what rainbows meant in my life. It is interesting how God brings confirmation into the picture when He asks us to do something.

As I prepared for the trip, I kept praying John 3:30: let there be more of Christ less of me. Whirlwind came to mind, and I found myself praying that truth descend like a whirlwind. Truth must set the groundwork to accept the Light of Christ. Darkness hates light, John 3:20– 22, for it fears exposure of its evil deeds. Four of us began the trip, myself being the only woman. We would be joined by three ladies on the second half of the trip, one of which was my daughter Faith who was seventeen at the time. India was our first destination, and after a layover in Delhi, we're on our way to the city of Kolkata. The flight was fairly uneventful, and the only thing I felt God had taken me to was Joshua 10. When I read it, I did not see how it pertained to the trip at that point, but the Lord did not release me from it.

When we landed at the Kolkata airport, we were first welcomed by a twenty-foot Cali statue, a reminder that we weren't in Kansas or Indiana anymore. We quickly found the pastor who had come to pick us up. We arrived during the summer again and were welcomed by sweltering heat. They took us to their daughter's home for lunch and a review of our agenda there. We were trying to accomplish a lot on this trip, and we really had very limited time. We were going to be there only a couple of days, and they wanted us to see as many parts of their ministry as possible, including one part that would require a seven-hour train ride one way.

Well, if you remember, my last time in India was not great for me health wise. I had been the lightning rod for spiritual attacks. I was hopeful and prayerful this would not be a repeat. When we got to their daughter's home, it was an apartment on the fourth floor, and there was no air-conditioning or air flow in the stairwell. I was fine the first two flights, but then, my asthma kicked in. By the time I was at the fourth floor, I was in trouble. I could barely breathe, the heat made me nauseated, and I started feeling anxious, like an anxiety attack. Really? Again? They ushered me into the one cool room in the apartment to see if that helped. As my asthma settled down and I could catch my breath, the anxiety improved. The nausea and headache were worsening. They had gone to great lengths to prepare a meal, and I felt obligated to eat some. It tasted wonderful, but I ate very little, as I did not want to add fuel to the fire.

We left there, and they took us to the red-light district, where the pastor's wife had a ministry with women trying to get out of the sex trade. Unfortunately, I was on a downward spiral and continued to lose ground. Desperately, I wanted to stay engaged; this was why I came. As we wound our way through the very close buildings, there were bloated, hairless dogs lying on the cobblestone. There were feces everywhere, some dog and some human. The heat, sights, and smells did not help the nausea and headache. We had to climb a couple flights of steps to get to a workshop, which is where there was a ministry trying to provide jobs to get women out of this lifestyle. They wanted to share with us their mission and vision, and my head hurt so bad I could not keep my eyes open.

Lord, help me here! It is so frustrating when you know prayer is the answer, but you can't pray. Then, as I was sitting on the stairway, trying to hold it together, my eyes closed, and I continued to call out to the Lord. Then I opened my eyes and saw a blue tint over everything. And when I closed my eyes, I still saw blue, Cali blue. That was the source of my sickness. There was some darkness connected to that statue, and it was causing oppression or some type of attack against me as I went by. Now knowing the source, I could start being strategic about praying to break it. Feeling as bad as I did, I really needed help to break through this attack, and everyone else was trying to gear up for the evening departure on the night train.

The group did not feel it was wise for me to go, so after leaving the red-light district, the decision was made to put me up in a hotel for the night, where there would be air-conditioning. The rest of the group, the three men who were my travelling companions, the pastor and his wife, would get on the train for the seven-hour ride. Even though I truly wanted to go with them and was feeling a little better, I was not yet well, and I sensed I was not supposed to go with them. I also felt the pastor's wife should not go either, but I didn't feel comfortable telling her that.

When I got to my room, I was locked in, and they did not want me to leave the room until they returned to get me, which would be late the next day. No windows to open for airflow or sunshine, and locked in was a little stressful, but I got on the phone and was able to get through on my phone to Eric. I told him what was going on, and having gone through enough of these spiritual battles together, he prayed over me, sending my forgiveness to the perpetrator of this curse and attack. Immediately after his prayer, my headache left, my nausea left, and my strength returned. A little while later, there was a knock on my door; it was the pastor's wife. She prayed about it and felt she was not to go with them. She felt there was something we were to do the next day while the men were gone. My spirit was in agreement. The enemy intended this for harm, but once again, I knew God would use it for good. I was not staying behind because of the attack but because God had a plan.

Feeling better and after she left, I ventured around the corner of the hotel. I was on the block where Mother Theresa lived and ministered. There were still sisters carrying out the work she started. I was

IT'S ABOUT HIM

able to go in and listen to their service and pray with them, what a humbling experience. She had gotten it; blessing others and stepping into their world and pain brings fullness to life, which nothing else can. You cannot help but respect and admire that level of sacrifice and dedication. As I prayed in that place, my prayer was that Christ alone be the center of what went on there, that all work was for His glory and God's kingdom.

When I went back to my room, I read Joshua 10 again, prayed, and went to sleep. The next morning, they moved me to a room in a guest house, which would be less expensive for me to stay in, and the guys would join me there in the evening. The pastor's wife brought me some fresh fruit, and I have never tasted such a wonderful mango or banana. Never have I eaten anything more satisfying. We left there and headed to the slums. She shared how they use to live in the slums so they could minister there. Her husband had given up a good job working for the utility company as an engineer, feeling called to go into ministry. The pastor's wife was born into the Brahman caste, the one of wealth and influence. They both had sacrificed a life of comfort for the gospel.

As we arrived at the slums, I drew attention. My complexion was not the typical, and this area was primarily Muslim. Our source of transportation was a trike. I cannot remember the name for it, but a man pedaled the trike and we sat on a bench seat behind him, through the streets of the city. It was like taking your life into your own hands, with all the cars buzzing by you, lots of honking, and there was no being incognito.

The slums were shocking. The structures were poorly built; there were piles of garbage in the streets, with dogs eating out of them. The home we went to visit was that of a widow, who had her family living with her. I would guess the room to be about seven feet by nine feet. She had a small burner and basin at the entrance, which was her "kitchen." You stepped down into a room which was almost completely taken up by the "bed" which you climbed up on to sit or lay if you were going to sleep. It was about three to three and a half feet off the ground. It was up this high so a second layer was formed underneath so family members could sleep under and some on top of the bed. She had a small cabinet and various things hanging on the walls since there was very little storage. It was very clean. There was no bathroom. She was a gracious host.

We had a Bible study, and we sang and prayed together. I was asked by several ladies to please come pray a blessing over their homes and families. One very beautiful young wife, who had converted from Islam to Christianity, was four months pregnant, and she asked me to pray for her that she would be a godly mother and that she would raise the baby up in the way of the Lord. Lord, I am not worthy. What a privilege to be welcomed into these homes and these lives. These women were a light for their families and their community, living in the hard places, loving and blessing those around them; out of their poverty they gave.

There was one exception. When I looked at her, I did not see the light of Christ. It was important to know her story, so I knew how to pray for her specifically. I came to find out she was setting up camp in every camp to make sure she covered all of her bases. She was going to a mosque, a Catholic church and a protestant church, and temples seeking to follow everything. I shared that by standing on the fence, you did not really belong to any of them, and it becomes a place of loss and a trap. I assured her that Christ was enough, she didn't need to make it complicated; He has been faithful and trustworthy my whole life. There was so much to learn from them, and yet they wanted to learn from me. Hopefully, God was pleased, in that I believe we learned from each other. It was getting late, and we headed back to the dormitory. We had completed our assignment.

The guys returned with stories of their own. They had gotten to go to a Muslim village where a Christian man had started a school for the children there. What they did not expect was 42 percent of the beautiful young teenage girls were sold by their families to men promising a revenue stream for the families, while they were used in sex trafficking.

Many of the very sad women I had met the day before in the red-light district did not choose that lifestyle, they were sold into it by their parents. Lord, may I not judge these people but be broken by the poverty and conditions that would bring people to sell their children, their daughters to be used and abused. Forgive them, forgive us. Break my heart with what breaks yours, this breaks us all.

My prayer is that the Lord change the culture which does not value life, that does not protect the purity of children but steals it, that feeds the lust of men, worships things of this world instead of the Creator. Forgive us. It may not look the same in America, but the heart of it is exactly the same. You ask why go beyond our borders, this is why. I cannot stay the same after being in this place. I have to confront and step into the battle for these lives; it may be in prayer, it may be in ministry, but, Lord, let it change me to be more like you.

Chapter Fifteen

The Buddhist Kingdom of Bhutan

As we were on our way to the next leg of the adventure, Bhutan, we joked and laughed at how fully engaged and alive we felt. If we could only harness this vitality and energy and passion when we got home and back into the daily routines of life. Bhutan is a kingdom, a Buddhist kingdom. I don't think there are a lot of those left. The king of Bhutan is a man who was educated in England, and he considers himself enlightened. He observed that the capitalist society did not seem to fulfill people and make them happy, so he decided that monitoring financial status was not a good gauge to measure by. So, as we landed in Bhutan, and the plane banked hard and landed in a valley between the mountains, the first thing I saw on the side of the runway beside the terminal building was a billboard with picture of the king and queen and the statement that they measure the gross national happiness.

The architecture is beautiful, the scenery is beautiful, the river was crystal clear, the sky was brilliant blue, and there was darkness. Not the kind you see with your eyes, but that you feel in your spirit. They were boasting about their happiness index, yet there was fear behind every set of eyes I looked into. We were met by our guide, who was of Nepalese descent. He was also a pastor. The government knew about it, and as long as they did not disrupt things, they were allowed to gather. There was, however, an understanding that every home, every business, every gathering place had better have a picture of the king and queen in a place of prominence; they could be checked in on at any time, and their ability to gather could be altered at any time. It was their normal. It was not, however, our normal.

I only knew a little about the Buddhist faith. Teaching Sunday school, we had done sections on world religions with the middle school, and I knew the basic history of Buddha and the tenets of their religious system. We were taken to a museum shortly after we arrived. There were all kinds of ritual masks and tankas. The masks have a lot of dragon faces, bulgy eyes, and some with sharp teeth, all looking menacing and dark. Tankas are like a wall hanging in which religious scenes or inscriptions are placed on them, and they are to be meditated upon until they "come to life." If they focus well and long enough, they become three dimensional, and a spirit will come out of them and commune with them.

Then they had different statues and likenesses of Buddha. Truthfully, the masks and statues seemed to mix animistic religion with the worship of Buddha. One such representation was graphic and vile, with the foot of Buddha on the necks of people. One person in our group was so creeped-out by this version that they kept talking about how much it got to them.

We went to our hotel, which was absolutely beautiful and pristine, even though we specifically requested modest accommodations. It is the tour guide's responsibility to make a good impression on visitors, and the fees paid for your visa to get into the country include accommodations, food, travel, and all expenses. They are checked on to make sure the monies are spent well in making guests happy. He did not put us in the nicest facility, but also could not put us in an inferior one. When we got to the hotel to settle in, each of us had our own room, and the one who was "spooked" by the Buddha turned on the lights when they entered their room and the bulbs exploded and shot toward them. They promptly left and stayed in the room with one of the other travelers. Their fear grew.

During the night, the Lord was moving. God did not let me sleep. I prayed and read my Bible and listened to my Christian music. I worshipped and sobbed and prayed all night. The Lord was revealing things so quickly and with so many layers it was hard to take it all in, it was like a whirlwind . . . oh, that is what that was about.

When daylight came, I knew I was to fast that day. This was the day the Lord brought me here for. There was a tangible excitement in the air for me. What was the Lord up to? I sensed the guys should fast too, as this was going to be a battle day. When I went to get the guys, they had already gone down and eaten breakfast without me. It still seems strange that they did not even knock on my door, or maybe they did and I was so deep in prayer I didn't hear them. After breakfast, the guys came to my room for morning devotions and prayer.

I was given the gift of tongues when the battle became so intense with the work with Liz. I had not been raised in a church which actually ever talked about it, and the church I go to now does not either; however, during the very heavy battle time, a dear friend approached me and told me the Lord wanted me to acknowledge and accept the gift of tongues. It would help me in the battle I was engaged in. Praying in the Spirit has been very helpful in breaking through spiritual strongholds, and there are times I know it is necessary.

As we gathered that morning, I shared with the guys that God had been working all night and that today was going to be a day of spiritual warfare. I began to pray and sob, and I sensed the need to be on my face, prostrate before the Lord, not the typical in the Quaker church, but I needed to pray in the Spirit. As I prayed, in between the sobbing came a travailing prayer, something I had never experienced. The sobbing would ebb and flow, but the sobs came from the depth of me. I sensed that God was "birthing" something into this nation through me. As I prayed, He gave me a vision of the world. It was like a giant round dry dirt clod, dusty, it was so dry, and there was a black band around it, choking the life out of it.

God had shown me a vision of the world that was scary, but I sensed a hope; God is not done with us. He was showing me what we were fighting, but not what we had to settle for. This was the battle, break through the death grip satan has on the world. Now I don't know how big the army is fighting this battle. The Lord may be giving this assignment to hundreds or thousands or maybe I am the only one, it does not matter. What matters is that I am obedient with what

God has for me, period. I cannot get caught up with comparing and seeking out the "what ifs." It is not my battle, it is the Lord's. Christ won the war, but satan is not giving up until the end. God wants us to be engaged, and He is waiting for His people to step into the battle for the world, for the souls, for the people He does not want to see satan steal away.

One of the team shared that the Lord had given him Revelation 3:7–8, referring to the key of David which opens a door no one can shut and can shut a door no one can open. Our prayer became one in which God would close the door on darkness in this place and open the door of light which no one could shut.

After we finished our prayer time, one of the guys came up to me and said he had a dream before we came that God was going to birth something through me on this trip, and he was going to witness it. Yes, it was crazy; it seemed crazy to me, and I was caught in the middle of it, but God confirmed what He was going to do before He did it though this man's dream. It encouraged me and him.

At this point, we were getting ready for our day's travel. The Lord told me I needed to ask each of the guys individually if they wanted to be a part of what God was going to do that day and to let them know we were headed into battle. It was their choice; again, He is a gentleman. We were going into battle, and nothing is worse than being caught in enemy territory and realizing you have been pulled into a battle when you thought we were going to go on a joy ride. We needed to all be on the same page. Two of the three were "game on." The one who had been hijacked by the spirit of fear was still being hijacked. He thought we were going to die that day, he was not sure what he was getting into, and he was hesitant to commit. What I knew was God was in control. God had a plan, and whether we were all in or not, He would do what needed done with those engaged.

Timing, God is the Great Conductor, and I know this, yet I am still surprised by how He orchestrates things. As we started up the mountains, we saw hundreds of people on their pilgrimage to the various temples along the way. We came to find out it was one of two high holy days on their calendar, and we were headed up the mountain with the destination of the King's Temple, actually The

High Temple of the King of Bhutan. Now I didn't know that was where we were heading, nor did I have any clue about their holy days or their calendar, but God did. He is amazing. Sometimes I wonder what I have missed out on when I got so busy and caught up in the rut of day-to-day life. When you see how He works, you want to be a part of it every day; but with kids, and work, and bills and . . . it seems hard. That is why we have to stay intentional and invest every day in the kingdom, every act done to bless others blesses God and furthers the kingdom. You don't have to be in the Himalayas on the other side of the world. Let God use you to share the love of Christ where you are. All of life is ministry.

As we travelled up the mountainside, we learned more about their religion. We learned about dharma, which is the account of good deeds and positive energy you have. You can pay it forward for yourself or another family member or pay it back to allow a family member to get out of spiritual debt. Now, that may be a simplification, but was at least my interpretation of it. There were thousands of prayer flags going up the mountains; they kind of reminded me of the pennant strings you see at a car dealership, very colorful, with prayers printed on them. This was a way to make deposits into your dharma account. As we travelled and learned more about Buddhism, it was more than a little disturbing finding that they put bodily fluids from the high priest into the incense, wafers, and holy water. There is no waste of any kind disposed of and not recycled back into the system, whether they are alive or dead. We would stop and pray as we went up the mountain at strategic sites, often feeling a specific scripture was called for to bring truth, healing, or release, and we would write it and leave it at the site, typically burying it so it would not blow away.

One spot we stopped at, we could see smoke rising from the forest a bit away; it was the silent village. The silent village is a place where people go who want to get mega returns of dharma for themselves and their families. People are very proud to be able to say they have a family member at the silent village, it offers prestige.

From what I gather, the most obvious attribute is that no one is allowed to speak there; it is silent. There are basically two groups of people there: a few to provide food and water and dispose of waste and those who have signed a contract. Those who have signed a contract have done so for a period of twenty to thirty years. As a part of their agreement, they cannot talk, they cannot cut their hair or nails. They are locked in a very small room with a wooden door which is locked from the outside; exchange of water and a flour or sugar paste, which is their sustenance, or for any body waste, is done by pushing under the door or through a thin slot. They exit in one of two states, death or completion of their contract. Many depart in the first state.

I have pondered this. And, well, it breaks my heart, it breaks God's heart. It is like working and sacrificing your whole life to earn money to get into heaven, only to find out you were paid in fool's gold, and it has no value. As I have pondered their condition, I prayed. I continue to pray for the Holy Spirit to minister to them in their isolation, to illuminate the darkness, and to reveal truth to them. The Lord will visit people in their dreams to reveal Himself; it is happening a lot in the Muslim world. So I pray that Christ will appear in their dreams, that the lies they have believed would be uprooted and seeds of truth would replace them. I pray that they not perish alone and lost.

When we neared the King's Temple, we were in the clouds, as if near the barrier between heaven and earth. Upon arrival at the King's Temple, our driver stood outside, and we took our shoes off and entered. There was a row of monks sitting in a row facing the very large Buddha idol. There was a mound of food offerings, since many were on pilgrimage there. They offered holy water and wafers, we politely declined. The others were drawn to the war room; it was full of weapons which had been used in battle.

I stood in front of the idol and declared there is no God above the living God Jehovah. I then faced the thrones and paintings of the king and declared Christ is the king of all kings and there is none above Him. I prayed to God, in the name of Jesus Christ, that His Kingdom, the only eternal and true kingdom, come and that this pale reflection of a kingdom be revealed for what it was.

The others came around as I prayed and claimed that Christ is Lord of all and that it was His sacrifice that paid the price and that there is no other god than the Creator God, God of the universe, and that this anchor point be broken by the power and authority of Jesus Christ, and I was to stomp my foot. I was not sure what an anchor point was, but I was obedient. I could not see anything physically change with this proclamation, but in the Spirit, the vision was radiant light shining through a crack in the floor from the foundation.

We exited the temple, and I felt led that I was to pray and walk around the exterior seven times. Nothing was said, we just all went about our business or assignments. As I walked, I prayed that the walls and layers of deception be broken, that walls of protection for God's Truth would replace them, that the false foundation of Buddha crumble and be replaced with the foundation of Christ for this nation. When I was finishing my fifth lap, the driver started getting anxious, and he said that we had drawn enough attention, that with the cameras and guards we needed to get out of there. I acted like I didn't hear him and started my sixth lap, wondering how I would pull off number seven.

Then the one who had the dream about God birthing something stepped alongside me. I was a little caught off guard. He leaned over and said, "God told me to walk this lap with you and he is counting mine as the seventh." At times, you have to wonder, am I hearing this right? I always try to verify and weigh what I believe to be what God is saying to me, but what a blessing when someone else confirms what you heard without any foreknowledge. God is amazing. We did not dawdle but finished our lap and headed to the van.

As we debriefed on our departure, the Lord had given one a scripture to slide in the cracks of the walkway, which was hollow underneath, suggesting that what we saw inside the temple was not all that was there. My spirit sensed evil and darkness below us, and I had prayed over that during my laps. We listened to music and wondered what had just happened in the spiritual realm. We sensed we had completed that assignment. For all of us, it is about the lost being freed and coming to a saving knowledge of Jesus Christ, that the spirits of fear and control be bound, that people would not buy the lie that happiness is the prize and goal of life, but it is about wholeness and forgiveness, joy and peace that can only be found through Jesus. That was the message for Bhutan—wait, that is the message for the world!

We had the privilege to meet with some of the house church leaders and heard their stories of the miraculous, from healings and casting out of evil spirits, and the best of all, the transformed lives. They went from hopeless to hopeful. Because of the possibility of a plant or spy in their midst, they are very cautious about bringing people into the church. They start in house churches, and if someone expresses a desire to step into the Christian faith, they are discipled.

We departed Bhutan and headed back to India, Delhi specifically, and we then headed to Kenya. We had been getting partial information as there was interference on phones, but what we did get was that the three joining us, who were travelling separately because of timing and tickets, did not meet up at the right time and place. And Faith, my seventeen-year-old, might be left in Nairobi a day early by herself, with no one able to pick her up, because we could not get a hold of anyone on the Kenyan side to give them a heads up.

We also got word that there had been a tornado touch down at the Fort Wayne Airport near the time they were supposed to be flying out, so they might not have made their adjoining flights. This might not be a big deal in other situations—you know, you lose a day or so on a couple weeks' vacation, you adjust—but we only had a few days, and there were meetings and trainings, which people were coming from fairly far distances to reach in Uganda, and it would be next to impossible to adjust. Of course, for me, as the mother of a young lady who had never flown out of the country to be potentially getting to a strange place and no one knowing when she would arrive, and who with, could be a big stressor. What do you do when all the plans fall apart and potential misdirections happen, you can't communicate to verify anything? You pray and trust, of course.

We had no idea what was going on, who was where, when they would get where, how to arrange transportation, but God knew. Just the kind of game the enemy would play to distract us from our purpose and focus. Nope, we chose to trust Him in spite of the situation.

We boarded our flight with many more questions than answers. It was a night flight, and I don't sleep well on planes. My neighbor was Kamal. He was Indian, in his midtwenties, lower caste, a computer specialist, and heading to South Africa, if I remember correctly. Anyway, we talked off and on all night. We had some great conversations, and we talked about his Hindu background and the questions he had about it and its validity, the questions he did not feel comfortable discussing with his family or other Hindus. Questions about absolute truth and creation. We talked about families, faith, careers. It was a divine appointment.

The flight was over too soon in regards to our conversation. I had my Bible with me, and I wondered if I should give it to him. I hesitated as I was on a mission trip, and if I gave it away, I would not have it for the second half of the trip. I decided that was crazy, he needed it more than me. I then reached for it as we stood to leave, but when I turned back, he was gone. How I hated that I hesitated. Then when I got into the airport, he found me to thank me for our conversation. Then someone said something and I looked away, and again, he was gone. Lord, I missed my second opportunity. How frustrating, I am so sorry. I was trying to juggle my bags when my big bag or purse dumped out all over the floor. You have to be kidding! I bent over and started to pick things up as people were passing by in the crowd, then I realized someone had stopped to help. I looked up to thank them, and it was Kamal. I told him thanks and not to leave, I had something for him. I told him that this book held the answers to his questions and that it was not like any other book he had ever read, it is a living thing which speaks to you where you are, it is a love story of God to man, and I wanted him to have mine. He was shocked and took it bowing and thanking me. My prayer was and is that the seeds planted during our conversation were watered and nurtured by the living water of God's Word. Redeeming the lost opportunities, the mistakes, the misdirections, the distractions—that is what God does daily: God is the redeemer of all things.

Well, now it was time to regroup and try to find out who was where and when they got there or if they got there. We got some SIM cards for our phones and started making calls. We discovered that there had been a tornado, and it delayed the flight out of Fort Wayne, but in the end, the three ended up on the same flight and it was arriving at Nairobi Airport in like fifteen minutes. We ran to the gate, and I was there to greet my daughter. God had brought order out of chaos, and what couldn't be done when we booked flights happened to get them all there at the same time, and not at any time but the perfect time. Have I mentioned God is amazing and He cares about details?

Chapter Sixteen

Two Sides of Mt. Elgon Kenya and Uganda

Here, our group separated; three were heading to do training in Uganda, and the rest of us were heading to a place called Mount Elgon. Here, we would be meeting to do some strategizing and community assessment work. We, Faith, and two of the men, flew on a little plane, not the smallest I've been on but much smaller than the others on this trip. We flew to a little airstrip at Kitale. We were greeted by a gathering of about half a dozen people.

They were so excited to see us, and they were taking us to the church to have a meal. It was our first Kenyan meal, and they had gone all out. They also did not want us to leave hungry. They were the sweetest and most hospitable people I have ever met. You just fell in love with them and their hearts. They spoke of their desire not just to be receivers anymore but to be senders for the gospel.

After our meal, we were all exhausted and ready to go to bed. They took us to the home of one of the couples from Kitale, and we were there for the night. We drove into what I thought was the garage, but it was a multipurpose room. The vehicle fit inside, and there were three or four couches along a section built up a few feet up from the level of the vehicle, and a little table against the wall with some chairs. We visited a bit and were ready to go to bed. When we arrive, they wanted us to have some tea. We agreed, but it was another minimeal. We were about to bust.

We visited a little more, and then we went to our rooms to settle in, and we were asked to come out for another round of tea. We were not in a position to refuse, so we sat to have more tea, and she brought out yet more food, you know, for our midnight snack. What do you do but express your appreciation and realize "tea" to them is code for "extra meal," not the same as it is for us.

We went to our rooms in which there were three or four bedrooms in this hall. But unlike one of our halls, there was a door at the end and we were locked in. Momma Joyce whispered in my ear, "Sleep well, we have an armed guard watching over you during the night." My first thought was, "Oh great, we are in a place that requires an armed guard." The mental picture of the guards we saw at all the international airports with machine guns popped into my head. Well, I chose not to share this information with anyone else. Not sure it would help them sleep, it didn't help me.

We awoke the next morning, and she had prepared breakfast; and just like the tea that was not just tea, she brought porridge, fresh fruit, eggs, tea, and a course or two of other food courses. Suffice to say, we all looked at each other, eyes bulging. Here I thought I might lose a few pounds going to Kenya, and that would be fine by me, but instead, they were going to have to roll all of us home.

Faith looked outside and asked who the man was standing around with a machete. "Oh, him, he was our armed guard last night." Wish I had gotten a picture of her face. We left the hospitality of these dear people to be joined by some of the people from the night before and to get on the road to our destination, a place called Kaptama.

As we rode along, the director for the area said he had been given a vision of Kaptama being a beacon of Christ on the side of Mount Elgon. He shared how this people group had survived what was almost a genocide just a few years before. Many were killed when a group came from further up on the mountain down out of the forest to raid, kill, and try to claim the fertile farmland of the Sabaot Tribe. There were many children who were orphaned, and when the government came in to take control of the situation, they rounded up, beat, and jailed every man they could find, victim and perpetrator alike. Some were killed at the hands of the government. There had developed a fear and distrust from the injuries and losses, but the director felt this place was meant to be a place of peace, renewal, healing, and revival. He felt it was a place in which investment was needed.

What I did not fully understand was the significance of what was going on here. You can see racism in action, when those involved are different colors. From the outside, it is not obvious that there should be hatred within the same race. I guess satan uses anything he can to create division, using our pride and sinful nature against us. The director was a member of the Luhya Tribe, as were the people there from Kitale, and the Sabaot Tribe was not a tribe that they as Luhya would want to associate with. So this was God at work in their hearts to see these people as brothers and sisters in Christ, not tribal rivals.

Once we arrived at Kaptama, we visited the healthcare center there. It was in disrepair: the bed linens were gray; there was no equipment, well, no operational equipment; the microscope was broken; the autoclave for sterilizing was broken; and the centrifuge was a hand-crank unit that had four plastic test tubes attached to a pencil sharpener, really. That was the extent of the equipment. No, I forgot, they had a propane powered cooler for medications and vaccinations.

This was good, as they had sporadic electrical power at best. They did have a good stock of AIDS medications in which the government provided. They did not have a doctor on staff; they had a nurse who did the medical procedures. They delivered babies there, it cost, I think, sixty dollars, they said. Of course, the rusty and flimsy cots they provided to lie on during delivery were scary. The ground was that red-orange color, the color of the dirt on the ground, and the walls were tinged with that color from about eighteen inches down, I assume from trying to mop the floors and slopping the water up on to the walls.

They did not provide food for those under care in the facility, friends or family would have to go find it on their own. The challenges with that were seen in the situation that was present while we were shown the facility. There was a seven-year-old girl who had been raped, her mother had carried her two days to get to the center, and she had to leave her alone to try to find something for her to eat. She was cowering under her covers as we went on through the ward. Shortly after, I realized we had lost Faith; well, not lost, but misplaced her.

Someone said they saw her stay behind with the little girl. She sat on the edge of her bed, held her hand and prayed over her. The little girl did not know any English, but it did not matter. When Faith lifted her head, the mother had come in and was standing at the foot of her bed with tears running down her face. The miraculous happens when we are willing to step into someone's pain. She hugged the little girl and caressed her forehead. Where mercy exists, so does God.

We left there and, over the next couple of days, headed to multiple schools and met hundreds of children. As we were on our way up the mountain, I opened the journal I grabbed for the trip and was trying to find the page I had left off on, and there on the page before me was a prayer. As I read it out loud in the vehicle, the director said how perfect that prayer was for this place, which had suffered such loss and needed reconciliation and healing and unity. He asked if I had just written it. I smiled and said no, I had written it about this place a year before; before I knew it existed and before I had any idea I would be here. the Lord had impressed upon my heart His heart for a place in Africa, and He had given me the words and insight to know how to pray for a people I did not know, in a place on the other side of the globe. He then brought it together by allowing me to put people and details into the picture that I did not have before.

We drove on very rough terrain to the end of the road; literally, we stopped in a field just before a large forest or jungle. As we stopped, we were near a small church next to a school. The kids saw us and swarmed the car; they thought that they were looking at mzukas or ghosts. They had never seen white people. On this journey, we would be in four places in which they had never seen a white person, but the shock was most noticeable here. They pressed in on the doors so we could not exit, faces smiling and laughing and eyes open wide. When they finally understood we could not get out until they stepped away, they started poking and touching us, some pinching; then they saw my eyes, and several shrieked, blue eyes were very strange to them.

This school cared for eight hundred children, and many were orphans from the attacks. There was still a joy and carefree spirit within them in spite of the experiences they had. One of the things which surprised me was that the government had come to the leadership of the churches, asking why they were not providing more religious education in the schools. Their premise was that the government's responsibility was to educate the students academically, but it was the church who was called to provide the religious foundation and instruction. It was seen as an expectation that the church would be involved in education. The church was in the process of finalizing a peace curriculum in response to that request.

Once we toured the school and met some of the teachers and administration, we walked across the field and had a worship service in the church, which was a kind of hybrid pavilion and hut. What a joy to be here worshiping, the singing and clapping and dancing. It blessed me, really blessed me. I again realized what I had many years before in Jamaica, worshiping in unity between nations and cultures is very precious.

It was here that I learned that the Bible had just been translated into the Sabaot language and the first printings were available but they had not been able to buy any yet. There had been a couple who I am friends with who had given me some money to use where the Lord led. So I gave the money to buy Bibles for the church and community. There was a need, and God had the answer; he laid it on the hearts of a retired couple in Indiana to give. Their act of obedience blessed many with God's Word in their own native tongue. God is good!

They spoke of the jungle at the edge as something to be feared, and when we asked how many people live there, they had no idea. When we asked if they went into it, they quickly said no; it was the place with wild animals and the unknown. A couple of us would have loved to just keep on going to see what was there, but the voice of reason prevailed; we had much more ground to cover. Maybe on another trip.

They had divided us up, and we were staying with an older woman named Rebecca. She had a house that her children had built for her, and we drank tea and ate in it, but she did not really fully live in it. She did all of her cooking in her hut, and it seemed she felt much more at home there. There was another small building with two beds in which three of us stayed in at night. There was no electricity, no running water; there was an outhouse and an out-shower stall (no plumbing). They had their milk cow, their chickens, and they grew their vegetables. Rebecca got up early and boiled water for bathing and making tea, and she made breakfast after she gathered her eggs, milked her cow, and had gone to get water. Her day was literally consumed with catching, cleaning, picking, and carrying, chopping wood for her fire, and growing food for her family. It was not an easy life, but it was blessed and much more focused and uncluttered than our lives. It was like stepping back in time. It was an honorable life, where everyone had to work together and look out for each other to survive. They were blessed to live in a lush land where crops grew well, not all of Kenya was like that.

We did visit a few more schools in the area, and then we reconvened with the church leaders, the community leaders, and our team. We were all at the same table talking about what the community needed, we strategized and established the outline of a plan. When we finished, they had us plant teak trees; each of those at the table had one to plant. This had been a historic event for them. It was the first time people from differing tribes and cultures had come together to figure out how to bless and move forward what existed on Mount Elgon in a little place called Kaptama. How humbling to be a part of this. Thank you, Lord.

Next, we were off to join the rest of the team as they finished their last days of training with the group of about twenty in Uganda. There were pastors there from the Congo, Rwanda, Kenya, and Uganda. They all came to find out how to be better disciples and followers of Christ and how to develop and implement business plans to be self-sustaining and to invest and engage in their communities. Their travel, accommodations, and training had been paid for with money raised at the Radical Auction I mentioned earlier. Out of our excess, we gave back instead of continuing to build our own kingdoms, and God was blessing this act of obedience. What else could we accomplish if we lived sacrificially. Only heaven knows.

We were able to visit schools in Uganda, but there was a difference; the kids did not display excitement or joy, some of the children had an absolute coldness and emptiness in their eyes. Now both areas had experienced violence, loss, and death, but how these children handled it was much different. Of course, it may have had to do with how long they were exposed to it, but it burdened my heart for these children, or maybe the strongholds of the enemy were impacting them. Pray for the children who have seen nothing but fear, hatred, and loss in their lives. Oh, how they need Jesus.

What a whirlwind of a trip, there was that word again. What a diversity of cultures. And the four of us who had been on the whole trip felt like we had been on this journey for several weeks, we had met so many people, seen so many ministries, schools, churches, historic and cultural sites, and had been on over a dozen flights, had worshiped together in four distinct cultures, learned about the vision and hearts of those leading the charge in these places of hardship and oppression, had been a part of a community assessment, planted trees, heard part of the training and the business plans of pastors from several African countries. We had come in contact with Muslim, Hindu, Buddhist, the occult practices of the animistic all within this less than a two-week timeframe.

It was like God had held back time, literally, to help us accomplish and experience all that we did. Do you remember me talking about Joshua 10? It is the story of when the Israelites are engaged in battle and the Lord let time stand still, the sun did not move, until they had accomplished what God had set forth for them to do. God is not bound by time, and every once in a while, when it serves His purposes, He allows us to experience that. We were fully alive, fully engaged, fully focused, and we had experienced the holding back of time.

Transitioning back to normal life is always a challenge. To come back from an experience like that and try to find the balance to not lose the momentum but to pace yourself as you re-enter a world that has no idea and cannot fully relate to what you have just witnessed. They say you will only have a very few you get to tell your story to beyond a three-minute synopsis.

That is one area I feel blessed in. I work one on one with people and spend an average of forty-five minutes with them two to three times a week, so I end up with a somewhat captive audience. The blessing is they ask, as they have gotten to know me and know I am travelling abroad; they seem genuinely interested in what God is doing around the world. So I get to share my heart and my stories over and over. My patients are some of the people who have encouraged me to put my story down in a book. It is hard not to let routine and daily stresses, which cause you to forget, or to get so busy you seldom dwell in that place of remembering how amazing the God we serve is, and He is fully engaged all the time, not just when we temporarily step into it.

You know, it is not a new problem. Have you ever looked at what God did for the Israelites when He rescued them from Egypt, brought plagues that did not touch them, parted the Red Sea, sent manna daily, yet look how quickly they got distracted and back into their own ruts again, the ruts consumed with themselves and what they wanted, forgetting to focus on the One who had proven He is worthy of our praise, our focus, our hearts, and our lives?

They did not even have the Holy Spirit residing in them. God resided in the Ark of the Covenant. After Christ came, that all changed, yet we still cannot get it right. We have to be shaken out of this trance we continually get lulled into. That is why it is required for us to be intentional about how we live. We are fooling ourselves if we think gravity is not continually affecting us physically and spiritually, it is always pulling us down and back, it takes that focus and determination to fight the status quo of contentment and comfort.

Chapter Seventeen

A New Phase in London and Atlanta

Within a few months, Faith was wanting to go to London. She loves all things British, including the bands. She asked if she saved up her money, could she go to England on spring break, this being her senior year. She had a few friends who had also expressed enthusiasm about this plan and had agreed to work toward making it happen. The stipulation was that they had to have an adult with them. One of her friends was from India, and she has family all over the world, and they travel often, so she thought that someone from her family would probably end up the chaperone.

Well, Faith was serious about this, and Eric and I had talked about it. I sensed I should take her, but did not want to interfere with her plans. As time drew closer to commit, her friends did not. She had worked since summer saving up for her plane ticket. We prayed about it, and both Eric and I felt she and I were supposed to go. She had saved up her money, but it was not in the budget for me to go, but knowing God has a way of providing when it is His plan, we prayed and waited to see what God would do. Well, He provided. One of Eric's aunts had left some money to her family, and a check to cover the expense of my flight and our accommodations arrived from the estate. So we booked the flight and found reasonable lodging. Her trip was on. I had committed to go to a prayer conference the day after our return from the trip, so we knew it was going to be a busy few weeks.

Spring break was here before we knew it. We packed and planned and were off on a different kind of adventure. She was going for a vacation. I felt I was on assignment, but did not know what it was going to entail. We got to London and to our hotel safely. We had our maps for the London Underground, our transportation, and a list of the places Faith wanted to make it to. I had been to London and Europe, but that was over thirty years prior, with our German and French clubs in high school, so I had been blessed to have seen many of the attractions, they existed even back then! We bought a London Pass, which allowed us to enter most historical sites and museums without additional charge. We went to Buckingham Palace, Trafalgar Square, Piccadilly, Tower Bridge, Westminster Abbey, Big Ben, British Parliament, the London Eye, the Tower of London, Kensington Palace, Windsor Palace, Kew Gardens, we took a cruise on the Thames, we stopped for tea a couple of times a day, we walked miles and miles and it was wonderful. There was just one problem: I loved being with my daughter, I loved seeing the sites, but what was my assignment. I had prayed numerous times, and I prayed as we walked all over London, asking God to reveal Himself, open eyes, soften hearts, break through strongholds; every church or cathedral we went in I would pray too. I knew He would let me know when it was time, but we were down to a few days.

We ended up at St. Paul's Cathedral as one of our last big historic sites. In the center under the dome, they had seats you could sit on, so I sat and prayed. As I sat there and prayed, the Lord told me there was something there that dishonored Him, and I needed to pray to break its hold. I reminded Him, this cathedral was huge and there were so many statues, crypts, levels, how would I know? He simply said, "When you see it, you will know." Then He said something I did not expect, He said this was another anchor point that needed broken. What? You mean there is more than one? What? Who knew? Well, He knew, and that was that. So I told Faith we had our assignment, and I told her what I knew.

We started walking along the side of the main altar area and ended up behind the altar. I looked down and saw a black-and-white marble pentagram. Now I did not feel it was the "something," but really, you couldn't have found a better shape to put in the floor behind the altar? There was a case holding a book with all the names of the soldiers who had died in battle in World War II, both American and British. I stood on the pentagram and just prayed over it. I didn't figure it would hurt. The funny thing is, Faith saw it also and nudged me because she didn't think I saw it because I was standing on it.

We stepped to go back along the other side of the altar area, and Faith and I both looked up at the same time and gasped. Yep, we saw it at exactly the same time, and we both knew. He was right, and I was actually a little surprised at how certain we were. Up in the ceiling was a masonic symbol, an actual Freemason symbol. Well, we prayed to break the web of lies connected with an organization which has been in plain sight all over the world and in almost every city in America, cloaked in secrecy and darkness. Evil cloaked in good deeds, and its tie to the beautiful cathedral really did dishonor Christ.

Well, after we prayed and felt released about that and about breaking another anchor point, we enjoyed the beauty and grandeur of the cathedral. We walked up to the base of the dome and went to the whispering walls. Faith then went all the way up, but with my asthma and the tight climb, I thought it wiser to wait for her. She said it was so steep and close that you could barely fit through and your knees hit the feet of the person in front of you, and your face was not at the best height either. So glad I didn't try it, there was no way to turn around, you had to keep moving forward.

We left the building, and like He often does, He tells me to walk and pray around the outside of the building, usually counter-clockwise, that way I am going against the flow of time. I don't know if it is significant, it's just how I feel that is the direction I should go. Well, when we got outside, the assignment was three laps. No big deal, we can get that taken care of in short order, or so I thought.

When I had gotten three-fourths of the way around the cathedral grounds, my asthma kicked in so severely I could barely complete my first lap. Well, Faith had walked with me, and we had been around the building just taking in the sights earlier, so I prayed and ask the Lord to please count the casual walking as one lap, Faith's as one and mine. My logic was that He had counted the last lap of a friend in Bhutan, it seemed reasonable. As soon as we were fifty feet away, I could breathe fine. I had already reasoned it out and justified my position, so we left.

Faith had bought a shirt about a block away from the cathedral, and on our way back on the Underground, we discovered the young man had double charged her, so the next day, we headed back to the area of St. Paul's Cathedral, and the Lord had not bought my justification, so I knew I needed to complete my other two laps. We got her refund and went walking and praying around the cathedral. Well, three-fourths of the way around, it hit me again, I could not breathe. Now I can push through pain and fatigue, but not being able to breathe stops me in my tracks. I had to get out of there. Once we were just off the property of the church, my breathing improved. What is up with this, Lord? You asked me to pray, and the enemy is keeping me from finishing. This is SO frustrating. Well, I once again asked the Lord to just count Faith's lap today as the third, because I was sapped and we were leaving in the morning for Heathrow Airport for our return home.

Feeling confident in the decision to head back to the hotel, we did and we got our stuff together and packed, except for the things we would need in the morning. We went to bed. After walking miles every day, we were getting a little tired, and I was looking forward to getting home to my honey and precious little girls. So I laid down to go to sleep and was praying through what had transpired over the week. It had been a great week. It was wonderful to have the time to talk and laugh and build memories. In addition to all that wonderful stuff, I had been able to complete my assignment for the Lord. All was well.

Then why was I not able to sleep? The Lord kept reminding me I was to walk three laps, and I had only completed two of them. He was not going to let this go. Argh! We had to leave for the airport before 9:00 a.m., and it took about forty-five minutes to get there. I had to walk several blocks to get to the Underground, then a transfer, and a couple blocks to the cathedral. I could not stand it any longer, it was almost five, and I needed to get going soon to make it back in time to not be too stressed for departure time to get to the airport.

As I was getting ready, Faith rolled over and asked what was going on. I told her, and she did the teenage "I don't have to go, do I? I am so tired." "Of course not" was my response. Now the idea of heading out in the dark by myself was not my favorite idea, but I knew the Lord would be with me. It only took a minute though and Faith was climbing out of bed saying she couldn't let me go alone. I chose not to argue the point, and in just a few minutes, we were heading out of the door so I could finish what I started. We got to St. Paul's and started my last lap. I assumed that the pushback would be over with that third lap, but once again, I barely completed it before my breath was taken away for the third time, but I did complete my lap and found a park bench not far away and sat down, thanking God for allowing me to be there, for not letting me leave before I completed what He had called me there for.

As I sat and prayed on the corner of the cathedral property, I heard or saw, "And next you will go to St. Basil's." Sometimes when the Lord speaks to me, I hear it in my spirit, but I can see the words, it works to kind of confirm what is not tangible or auditory. I was not expecting that. Really? There is another place? I had heard of St. Basil's but was not sure where it was exactly. As I sat and prayed, I realized that this is one of those times that the Lord allowed the enemy to have his way, his causing me to have to stop after each lap played into God's plan and purpose. It was supposed to take three days to complete, and it was actually easier to just let the enemy believe he was the one controlling the situation. Once again, what evil intends for harm, God will use for good. We stopped for tea and a pastry on our way back to the hotel to then head to the airport. The remainder of the trip was peaceful and uneventful. I love how God shows up when we take those steps of faith.

We got home in time for me to throw some clothes in the laundry, sleep, and hit the road. I was headed to Georgia for a prayer conference. A friend knows my heart and passion for prayer, and he recommended I go connect with others of the same heart, specifically

IT'S ABOUT HIM

with an interest in praying for Buddhists. I drove through Nashville on my way through but did not have time to stop.

Once at the conference, I met many amazing people who had invested their lives in trying to reach those trapped in the Buddhist religion. After my experience in Bhutan, I thought I knew some things about the faith, but boy, did I learn some significant things at this conference. For example, Buddhists do not believe truth is something which can be captured in words, so the Bible does not serve as a starting point with them. They do not believe in sin, a Creator, or one God. There are no absolutes, and truth is all relative. Their religion is like shifting sand, you just can't quite connect with them on any of the normal levels, which seem obvious to the evangelical Christian. So what do you do? Prayer becomes even more important because you need the Holy Spirit to help them see their need for God and a savior, to convict them of sin in their lives, and that there exists a firm foundation of truth found in the Word of God. We had some great prayer times, and the people were welcoming.

One of the ladies I met there was very interesting. She had given up her law practice, stability, and success to search for something more, to follow Jesus wherever He led. He had led her to Kansas City to the IHOP (International House of Prayer) where she had resided for some time. She was at this conference to pray and learn more about the Buddhist religion too, but her plan was to go and pray and meditate in Nepal and to live among the Tibetan refugees, trusting and stepping out in faith. Many would think she was reckless or crazy, but I have seen enough. I understand the draw to keep taking bigger steps to just see what happens when God shows up proportionally to our steps of faith.

She needed a ride back to Nashville, and I was heading that way, but I was looking for quiet and solitude, so I was not too excited to have a companion for that long a trip, but it seemed like the right thing to do, so I did. It offered a chance to hear her story and to pray with and for her for what God had planned for this lady. I dropped her off at the bus terminal. I continued to pray for her. I have no idea where God has taken her, but I know she is in His hands and He has the best grip. I love divine appointments.

Next, I was supposed to meet up with Marshall for church, but I could not get through on my cell phone to his. I sat in a park in my car in Franklin, Tennessee, for a couple of hours, trying to find where he was. I prayed about the interference which was keeping us from connecting. I had a seven-hour drive home from there, and I had just spent all the time I wanted to spend with him trying to find him. Well, I was about to give up and head home when I was finally able to get through to him. Church was over by then, so we decided to meet for lunch.

We spent lunch debriefing about the trip to London and this conference. Then I told him about what I believed would be my next assignment. My research had verified my thought that St. Basil's was in Russia, Moscow specifically. So when I told him I would be making plans to go to Moscow sometime in the future, when God directed and provided, he looked stunned. Then he said it had popped into his head about two weeks previously that he "needed to go to Russia." The thought caught him so off guard because he had never had any desire or thought about going there, but he could not shake the sense that he was supposed to go. When he heard what God called me to, he told me that he knew he was supposed to go with me. Now he understood why God wanted him to go to Russia, He was preparing him and confirming once again for me. What we did not know was God's timeline, but He was good about letting me know in ways only He can.

I prepared to head home, my head absolutely swimming with all that had gone on in the past week and a half. As I was driving home, I, of course, was talking to the Lord about what a blessed time it had been and how I appreciated how he made divine appointments, confirmed, and blessed as I took these steps of faith. I was just at 65 on the north side of Nashville; it was 5:30 p.m., and ahead and to the right was a rainbow. Wow! A reminder of God's promises and love. I love rainbows. As it started to fade, it became more of a pillar than a bow, but it stayed in the same spot no matter what way the road turned. This was strange; typically, a rainbow lasts only a few minutes at most, but this was staying the same distance as I drove. After about a half hour, I started calling my husband and then my kids telling them about this rainbow pillar which was still very vibrant and very much still there, I had never witnessed such a thing.

After I had called them all amazed, I would sing praises and pray, exuberant about what God had planned for the future, not that I knew exactly what it was, but I sensed the adventures were not over yet. Well, after an hour and it was still there, I had to call them all again. After two hours, I called again, and then at 8:30, it was almost dark and I could still see my rainbow pillar. It had been three hours. It then shifted to the left and faded away. I have witnessed some amazing things in my life, but knowing the rainbow is the radiance surrounding God and how He chose to make it a reminder of His plan, His promises, His faithfulness and His power, I was in awe of God and so thankful to know and serve Him. God is good, God is great, God is amazing!

Chapter Eighteen

The Desert

Now there have been awesome times that I hear the Lord clearly, and there are also times that He is quiet, like a dry spell. Those I am not so fond of, but just as God created the seventh day to rest, all things need those breaks `and rest periods. It is during those times we discover who we really are. It is kind of like the adage, character is defined by what you do when no one is watching.

How do we choose to live when we are not getting constant feedback? Do we continue to move forward trusting God's heart, trusting His consistency, trusting His Word, trusting His love for us? That is how I want to live, that intentionality does not change due to my situation. I can still step into hard places, into other people's pain or loneliness or fear. I can always choose to bless, I can also choose to be silent and wait for that still small voice. I know I am not alone, I know God is with me. I know He loves me. I choose to react to what God puts before me in the best way I know how. Might I make mistakes moving forward? Of course. But I have seen Him hedge me off, and I have seen Him redeem my mistakes. I always want to seek Him before I step, but in those quiet times, sometimes it is a test of faith. That is why He will eventually come back with "do you trust me?" That is the spell that happened between London and Moscow.

I was blessed to have the opportunity to go speak to a group of women and pastors' wives at a conference in India. I would be returning to Kolkata. This time, I was travelling alone. Well, just Jesus and I. It was the first time I would travel internationally, independent of a group, with someone else responsible to lead and make sure all the arrangements came together. London, I love, and Heathrow was not a concern; for one thing, everyone would speak English. The part that made me a little nervous was landing in Mumbai and having to get from the international terminal to the domestic terminal. I had been to the Delhi Airport a few times, and that would have felt familiar. Mumbai was new territory. The flight from Mumbai to Kolkata did not seem that intimidating either, as I had already been there, and the Cali idol and I had met, so I would be better prepared this time.

Well, the Mumbai Airport transfer was uneventful, other than it was very late and the exchange centers and SIM card offices were all closed. The flight from Mumbai to Kolkata was, however, the worst flight ever. Okay, in all fairness, we stayed in the air and landed safely, so it really could have been all kinds of worse; but in relationship to customer service, it was horrible. There was one stewardess for first class and a steward for the rest of us. Our gentleman was very grumpy, actually cold and rude. Once we got in the air, he informed us he would be coming around with complimentary water, and you could purchase beverages and food, but he did not make change or take cards; all I had was some American currency, which I had planned to convert over as soon as I landed, but I never saw anything open.

Well, I was thirsty, and the water would be good, but after he had poured two little cups of water and handed them to two people at the front of our section, he must have been offended by one of them because he became very angry and sat down, not to offer anyone anything the rest of the trip. It was not that long a flight, but I was so parched. Actually, I think it may have been the thirstiest I have ever been in my life. Maybe that is why they always provide beverages on flights, maybe the altitude dries you out. I always thought it was to distract you to make the flights seem shorter.

There was a twenty-something American young man who sat next to me. He was pleasant, but he had already taken life by the horns and had it all figured out. He was very confident and was happy to share his successes and his wealth of experience, which he had accumulated in all of his twenty years or so. Of course, he was the one sitting there with the orange soda he had brought and a sandwich, so he was definitely one up on me!

We landed and stepped off our plane in Kolkata, and I did not recognize anything. Even the Cali idol was not there to greet me, and neither was my friend, the pastor. They had built a new airport in the year and a half since I had been there, or moved into a new one, much bigger and more modern. There was a glass partition I walked back and forth along, but I could not find the pastor anywhere. Past the glass partition were the doors out. Well, so much for this being the smooth part of the trip. My phone did not have an Indian SIM card; they were not open yet in Kolkata either, and I had no Indian currency to pay to use a phone or to get a taxi. Wait, I did not even have the address of their home or church, so I could not take a taxi anywhere. My only other friends were in the slums and red-light district, and I didn't even know how to find them in those areas. After covering all the areas where you could see people waiting, I was getting a little concerned.

I started to go out to the area where the taxis were and shuttles, but the guard at the door looked intimidating with his machine gun. Thankfully, I asked him where else I might find my friend who was coming to pick me up, and he pointed to a painted line on the floor and said once I crossed it, I could not come back in. I took a giant step backward, I felt safer inside with him keeping people from coming in rather than being on the outside and him being the one keeping me out.

I did another perusal of the area and decided I needed to take my chances. As I neared the guard and I asked again where there might be people waiting to pick passengers, he said in broken English that there was a lobby area on the floor above, but he again cautioned me that once I crossed the line I could not go back. Well, I crossed the line and headed upstairs to the waiting area, and when I walked in, I realized it must be the only open public space in the airport, and there had to be at least two hundred men lying about sleeping or trying to sleep in this space, and I was the only woman. Even being only five-foot-four, I could not hide. Some the men were staring at me and talking between themselves, so I prayed for God to intervene; this was quite a predicament.

As I stood and prayed, the young American came through a glass door from the other side! He had been given a hall pass, which gave him permission to freely go between these two worlds; once again, he had that over on me too. I was so relieved to see a familiar face. He was in basically the same situation. He was trying to find an ATM to withdraw Indian currency so he would have rupees to get a taxi. He did, however, have enough rupees to make a phone call, so he would stop back by before he left to make sure I was ok. That was a relief.

Then I saw this door open and a woman behind a desk, and when the door closed, it said "Airport Manager." I knocked, and she allowed me to enter. I explained my situation to her, and she asked if I had my friend's phone number. I checked my phone, and I had his number from my last visit, so I prayed he still had the same number or I was up the proverbial creek. She graciously allowed me to use her phone, and when I dialed, the voice on the other side was a very worried male Indian voice asking, "Where are you? I have been looking for you for two hours." I told him where I was, and a happier greeting was not had by anyone at that airport that day, I am certain. God made a way where I could not see a way.

He was able to get me to my hotel, where there would be some other Americans coming in for the conference: the American director of missions and the international director of missions and his wife. The hotel worked out well and was about a ten-minute drive from the Christian college they rented facilities from for the meetings. We had at least seven nations represented, and what a blessing to sing and praise God together. What a privilege to be able to be a part of this gathering.

The theme of the meeting was Nehemiah 8:10: The Joy of the Lord is my strength. Of course, I had read Nehemiah several times but never really studied it like I did in preparation for this week of meetings. There was so much there; I would like to share what

THE DESERT

the Lord showed me and how it applies to us today. It was fascinating how God pulled it all together, how God used a man willing to step out in faith and risk his position and life to explain his burden for his people and country. First, it took his step of faith, and then God worked in the king's heart to make provision of protection and resources. How many times do we want the provision before we take any risk?

The temple had been rebuilt in Jerusalem, but the walls and much of the city remained in ruins. Nehemiah was a wise leader, and he gave each household the section of wall in front of them to build so that they could focus on something manageable rather than being overwhelmed with the daunting project of the whole wall, that could be intimidating or defeating; but if they focused on just their section, and their neighbor did also, each one doing their part, the end result would be completion of the wall. The other thing is, if the section of the wall you are working on protects you and your family, you would be very motivated to do it well.

I see some similarities with the body of Christ. God gives each of us a section of the wall, if you will, and if we do really well with it, he may give us a bigger section to work on. But me comparing my assignment to yours does not make the wall better, it distracts me and you from getting done what we have been called to. How often do we look at what task someone else has and wish it was ours, or maybe someone's gifts or talents? It takes all of us to accomplish what God has planned. Let us all work to accomplish the tasks set before us, using our gifts and talents to bless others and glorify God, trusting He has the big picture in His sights, so we just have to trust and stay focused.

The fact that the temple was rebuilt was great, but they did not do the work to protect it and complete the job of rebuilding the city. We see that with faith, people accept the gift of salvation and then sit in the middle of their brokenness content to stay amid the ruins; but just like God wanted the wall built to protect the temple and the people, if we don't allow the healing work of Christ to redeem and bring back to wholeness our lives, then we are like the Hebrews who sat in the ruins, not fully receiving the blessing that God was offering them. That is the life abundant that Christ is calling all people to.

In Nehemiah's day, there were those that mocked the things of God. They laughed at the thought that the Hebrews would even try to rebuild the wall. They began to listen and be discouraged, so Nehemiah had family members stand guard, to have their backs as you were, while they moved forward with their work. Their enemies became angry when they saw the work resume and were afraid, because without a wall, the Hebrews were not a threat to them, but with a wall, they became protected and whole.

Why do you think the enemy scoffs and mocks the things of God in our life? Is it to keep us among the ruins, because he knows that when God does restore us to wholeness, then we become a threat to his plans? Yep, I want to be a threat to his plans. I want wholeness. I want to be used by God. What about you? Do you need a Nehemiah in your life, someone to see the potential and know how to come alongside to protect you with prayer and encouragement? Then pray for God to bring that person to you. He will. He is faithful.

Part of the blessing of sharing at the conference was getting to reconnect with the people. Several of the brothers and sisters in Christ I had met in Bhutan were there, and those from my first trip to northern India, and of course, those leaders in the church in Kolkata.

After the conference was over, I was able to return to visit people in the red-light district and the slums. They were surprised when I remembered them and when I told them I had been praying daily for them. The world becomes smaller and less scary when you know faces and hearts; and the connections bring encouragement and hope.

Chapter Nineteen

A Fool for Christ
Moscow

Well, I had kept an eye out for good ticket prices to Moscow for nearly two years, wondering when God's timing would bring that trip together. All of a sudden, it did. My son Marshall was managing a couple of bands and was expecting a couple of weeks break between tours, I had a check arrive for vacation payout, the prices for tickets dropped to the lowest I had seen, and we still had time to submit for a visa into Russia. It was a little more complex than I had expected as other visas were basically making sure you had the paperwork and money sent to the consulate. This visa application was basically a paper interrogation, and our two visas came to almost six hundred dollars, and it was non-refundable if it was declined. You also had to have your hotel send a confirmation code to verify when you were arriving and departing, so you had to have your plans finalized before you applied. No pressure there!

As I was praying in preparation for the trip, I felt convicted that I had to fast from any of my mystery-type shows which dealt with solving murders due to the deaths involved or any violence. It was also important to spend extra time in God's word and prayer. The Lord always gives me scriptures to study before a trip, ones he will hold me on and not release me from. I will study the geography and history to help make better use of our time, sometimes there are clues in how to pray for an area based on these factors. Moscow was definitely a place where history and how the city was built played into prayer strategy.

I also sensed Marshall needed to be preparing too. He enjoys craft beers, and I sensed he needed to fast from all alcohol. I asked him to pray about it and not just take my word on it, and he just laughed, because he had drunk a beer while out with friends around the new year and had felt he should take a hiatus from drinking about three weeks before we had started making plans. So God had already laid the groundwork, and instead of him praying to confirm what I sensed, what I sensed confirmed what his spirit was already sensing from the Lord. I love it when the Lord uses confirmation to help us trust Him more and what we sense He is telling us.

Praying for confirmation wise, I trust the Lord implicitly, but I do not trust myself. I am human; I can be swayed by my own agenda, my own bents toward selfishness or pride. I am listening in the spirit, I have to make sure it is the voice of the Good Shepherd Jesus Christ I am hearing, not myself or some voice in my head seeking to create confusion or misdirection. As I went to the Lord in prayer about this trip and its timing, the Lord did speak to confirm. It was from a familiar passage, "I preparest a table before thine enemies, I anoint your head with oil, your cup overflows." I was relieved he didn't start a verse earlier, at "Even though you walk through the valley of the shadow of death . . ." Then there was the vision. It was rays of light beaming down specifically in one spot. As I concentrated, it was as if the light was causing a black billowing smoke to be displaced. As I prayed about it, I realized that it was a vision of light dispelling the darkness. That was then a prayer focus.

Next, I sought the insight of a friend from Russia about the culture and what to expect. She assured me that all the younger generation speak English and it is safer to approach someone younger, as they will not have as many issues and prejudices as some of the older people might. Knowing the years of distrust, I knew it could be interesting. Anytime I am travelling to a location that English is not the primary language, I try to learn some words connected to manners like "please," "thank you," "excuse me," "sorry."

My theory is that every culture appreciates manners, and even if I cannot carry on a conversation, my politeness may help break down the barriers connected to American brashness and rudeness, which unfortunately are world renowned. The other thing connected to the American label is "Christian," and sadly, that gets put into the mix with the less flattering adjectives. That is part of the reason much of the world puts up barriers to Christianity, because of its close connection to the politics of being "American." There have been places I have travelled that when asked if I am a Christian, I redirect to avoid the political attachments which follow the label. That is not to say I am not thankful I am an American; I look at all the good we have done in relief and rebuilding and protecting as a nation, but not all the world looks at our accomplishments through the same lens. I simply tell people I am a follower of Jesus Christ.

That is also why I don't like to answer with the label of a denomination. Man created these divisions, and choosing to accept that label over the label of a "follower of Christ" means I am accepting division in the body of Christ, and I choose not to. We have attended a Quaker church/meeting for many years, and even attended classes to join twice, but in the end, we felt we were not to take that step, as I have prayed about it. In my life, I feel I am personally called to reject those labels and align my allegiance solely to Christ. I love my church, I love the people in my church, but in the end, I am passionate about the Body of Christ. That is why I pray for unity in the Body; power is multiplied by unity, effectiveness is multiplied by unity, strength and protection are multiplied by unity. If you wonder why we, as Christians, are not usually seeing the miraculous on a regular basis, I truly believe it is due to our human pride and arrogance which has divided up the heart and power of the Body by dividing up the Body. God's word tells us that Christ left so He could leave the Holy Spirit behind. Did he say, "So you can kind of do some of the things" He did on earth? NO, He left so we could do even more (John 14:12). When I hear pastors support the thought that their denomination has the secret combination of doctrine that will get them in heaven and everyone else is lost, I rebuke that spirit of pride in the name of Jesus Christ.

IT'S ABOUT HIM

When I hear pastors and denominations decide which parts of God's Word they are going to promote based on their preferences and opinions or those of the world, I understand why Christ would say, "Get behind me, satan." God is calling us to a new age, a new anointing, and an empowering of the Body of Christ. When we return to what we know is true and right within the body, when we stand in unity under the Lordship of Jesus, that will unleash an outpouring of power and authority we have never witnessed. Christ is THE Way, THE Truth, and THE Life, no gets to the Father but through Him. He says when we call out on His name, we are saved (Ephesians 4:1–16, Unity in Christ).

Now back to the call to go to Russia to pray. We headed to Russia in late winter, before spring—God's timing, not mine. There was still some snow, and it was cold; I am sure not as cold it can get, but we went wearing our winter coats, scarves, hats, and gloves. While at the airport, we were able to get a map of the city subway system, so we felt confident about our preparation. Well, as confident as you can get when you are going to a country without really knowing their language, with a completely different alphabet, a history of war and hatred for America, knowing you know no one, also knowing that blending in would be good. But I am travelling with my son who is almost six foot-nine inches, he doesn't blend in very well.

You know the moment you realize you are out of your element. It was when we started walking through the airport and they had caviar dispensing machines and there was a lot of fur coats. In America, we dispense soda and candy bars; here, they have caviar machines. Nope, we were not in Kansas anymore. We, as on most of my trips, spent most of the money getting there and had to be wise about our cash. I had looked before we left to exchange some money into Russian currency but did not find it available out of Chicago, so when we got to the airport in Moscow, I had to get money exchanged.

We ended up at a hotel outside the city near the airport, as it was a more reasonable price, and they had a free shuttle service to and from the airport; therefore, upon leaving the airport, we knew to look for a shuttle from the hotel. We were thankful to have that part all figured out. We, of course, were tired after our journey and did not venture into the city the evening we arrived. When we awoke and headed down to breakfast, we were pleasantly surprised by the breakfast buffet with choices of several things we recognized. That does not always happen when you travel abroad. Things went well while we were in the hotel; they get paid to be polite to tourists. It was all well and good until we got to the subway station. Our map was translated into English, which we understood, but none of the signage had any English, so we stood there not able to make sense of either. We tried to speak to the younger people as we had been encouraged to do, but no one acted like they had a clue what we were saying; they just plain ignored us. When I tried to speak to the employees of the public transit system, they were cold and let you know that they did not want to be helpful. We found our way with the grace of God to Moscow, and we figured out we needed to make a transfer, so we approached a policeman in the subway station, showed him the map and pointed to where we wanted to go but could not find the entrance to; no language needed, but it did require a willing heart, which he did not have. He sent us the wrong way, when we were just on the other side of the wall from where we needed to be. We did find our way to inner Moscow and were already exhausted from the stress of it all. We had scheduled a free walking tour of Moscow in English, figuring it would help us get the lay of the land from the ground. Much of the history of Moscow and Russia was reviewed, and hearing it from a Russian, rather than reading about it, gave me a new understanding and appreciation for this nation. The guide started explaining that initially they were bands of barbarians until two Christian apostles came and united the groups under a common language and alphabet. Christianity was the foundation of the Russian empire. As we stood next to a statue for these two men, I thought how our nation had been built on a desire for religious freedom based on Christian principles. What difference was there on these two starts? This was something for us to ponder.

One of the struggles that has been a consistent problem for Russia is that their leadership, if good, gets overtaken, and those who don't get overtaken get crazy. Maybe it is that struggle with their sin nature and reverting back to the barbarism that was a part of their

IT'S ABOUT HIM

roots. Look at Ivan the Terrible, he was the one who built the beautiful St. Basil's Cathedral as a reminder of his conquests. He wanted the most spectacular building for his glory, and after building it, he asked the architects if they could reproduce it, and to be assured they could not he had their eyes gouged out. He was so ruthless and paranoid that he had his pregnant daughter-in-law killed so she could not bear another heir to his throne, and he killed his son. The interesting thing was that everyone was so afraid of him that they cowered at his presence, except for a man named Basil, a fool for Christ. He was the only man crazy enough to stand up to Ivan the Terrible and live through it. He was later named St. Basil, but this man was one who would go around naked or nearly naked; he was one who heard from God and performed miracles in the name of Christ. He, on two occasions, turned over carts, one with drink and another with food, and was arrested at the request of the cart owners. When asked why he did this, he said the Lord told him they were bad and would kill people and the quickest remedy was to overturn them. Both ended up being true situations, and he was released as a hero. When you look at the impact this man had on a time of great darkness and oppression, you had to respect him, even Ivan the Terrible did. St. Basil's was adjacent to Red Square and the Kremlin, and this was the seat of power for Moscow and originally Russia.

The next scary person to come to power was Stalin. Stalin started out in seminary to become a priest; he took a hard turn into atheism, but then counseled with mediums and sorcerers to determine the most spiritually powerful locations in Moscow. They reported eight, with one being the most powerful, that location being where the Cathedral of Christ the Savior was located. Stalin devised a grand plan. He wanted skyscrapers located on the seven high power spots, each with a big star at the pinnacle, and then a great monument in the style of a pyramid with a hundred-foot statue of himself atop it. The plan was that the power from these places of spiritual power would be funneled to his monument so that the power would raise him from the dead, as he would be entombed there upon his death. Well, he had the Cathedral of Christ torn down and the foundation laid for his great monument. When the war started and the metal to be used for the infrastructure was needed for the war, the foundation filled with water after the river flooded, and it looked like a great pool; so eventually, that is what they did, used it as a pool. His master plan never came to fruition, thankfully. When communism broke in 1990 in Russia, you would think after fifty years of being brainwashed that there was no God, that it might have worked, but the first thing the citizens of Moscow did was put together their resources to rebuild their great cathedral. It was reopened in 2000, a testament to the enduring commitment to their faith, which dictatorship and oppression could not squelch. It showed their hearts and their priorities.

Now on this grand walk we took, the guide kept apologizing for how far we were having to walk due to road closures because of the Defender of the Fatherland Celebration, a national holiday with a parade, military gatherings, and speeches. We entered some churches and one in service; there are no pews in their churches, you stand throughout the service or kneel or lay prostrate. Church is about discipline, perseverance, and sacrifice, not comfort like our sanctuaries. Head coverings are expected for all women, and an attitude of solemn respect was seen. Even outside in public, you do not see much joy, it is more stoic to angry.

The next morning, I awoke to "This Is the Day," and my response was, "That the Lord has made, and we will rejoice in it!" During our prayer and reading time, we felt a sense of expectancy, as we could sense a blessing or anointing on this day, and we were excited to see what it held. We went to St. Basil's first thing, as I knew my assignment was connecting to it. I walked and prayed inside the structure, a structure built on human arrogance, pride, and violence. It was originally named the "Veil of the Mother of God," which just rubs my spirit the wrong way. Mary was not the mother of God, she was the mother of Christ. To say she gave birth to God is absurd, and to put her in a place of deity and worship goes against the first commandment to have no other gods before Him. She was a chosen vessel deserving of our respect, but not our worship. This cathedral was not as ornate or grand on the inside as it was the outside. Set with the priority of man, make the outside beautiful, neglecting the inside where it counts. Looking at the example of Basil, a fool for Christ, willing to humble himself to make himself nothing so that Christ could work through him, he worked on his soul and had a connection with God that few ever experience, such a fool I want to be, so concerned about pleasing God that I can separate myself from the distraction of pleasing men. What I observed was a deep appreciation for the holy in the younger generation. I watched a young lady touch a picture of Christ and weep. As we walked within St. Basil's, they had a men's group singing a capella, filling the building with heavenly sounds. As I walked, I was praying confirming their God is our God, praying for walls and barriers to be broken, healing, and revival in this land. We walked and prayed around the wall surrounding the cathedral, then we walked up around the sidewalk of the building. As I walked and prayed that last lap close to the building, it came to me. Eric had commented on the structure of Moscow as he looked at a map, it was in concentric circles, like a bull's-eye. The path we took the day before because of the detours took us around a large circle, one we would not have made if it had not been the holiday it was, where the center was closed down and blocked off. We had made concentric circles from large to smaller, bringing Moscow back to its center, its heart, Christ. That was the physical journey mirroring what God wanted spiritually. As I completed my closest circle, the Lord told me I had accomplished what I came for, "it was done." Sometimes I think it would be so cool to see what is going on in the spiritual realm, but then it would not be faith, would it?

As we left St. Basil's we had thought we would go to the Kremlin, but as we headed to the entrance, we found it was closing in a couple of hours; we decided to wait until another day. We continued to walk, and I sensed Marshall was coming into his assignment. We kept walking and came upon the Cathedral of Christ the Savior. We were not sure the hours or accessibility, but decided we should check it out. We were so glad we did. It was breathtaking inside and out. Never have I seen more beautiful murals and scenes. As we walked and prayed, and were in awe of what was accomplished in this place to honor God, not man. We also prayed to break the curse that had been placed on the land, where, originally, a monastery and small church existed; the head monk was so angry that the cathedral was going to replace the monastery, he is said to curse it. This church was about restoring in proper order and place the things of God in this city, it was about victory over oppression and evil, it took sacrificial giving and unity in the body of Christ and the city. Again, we were touched by the devotion and reverence displayed by the youth who entered and wept. The Spirit of the Lord is tangibly present in that place. Marshall's assignment was connected to this place, and as we prayed and asked for confirmation as to what his assignment was, we realized he represented the new generation of Christians, and his proclamation of the victory in that holy place over the darkness complimented and completed our assignments. It was a day neither of us could put into words; it was a holy day set aside for the things of God to be put into their rightful place, to pray through strongholds and claim victory over a battle for a people who have experienced great oppression and heartache. Once we left the grounds of the cathedral, we both felt a release, our assignment had been completed. We rejoiced and celebrated all the way back to the hotel. We serve an awesome God who loves all people, even those we feel we don't have much in common with, or maybe the point is we do. God's timing is perfect. There had been building some political unrest in Russia, with Putin becoming more aggressive and controlling. Prior to our departure to Russia, a friend, whose family still lives in a Slavic country, shared concerns about the stability of the area, as they had been told about recent town meetings led by the Russians who were seeking buy in to reunite USSR, and those openly opposing were being threatened and punished. Upon our departure from Moscow, we left feeling excited about what God will do in this beautiful country with a long rich history, a culture and people God loves. When I asked my son what was the most significant outcome of this trip, for him it is his commitment to pray for the people there, something he would not have felt connected to do previously.

    When we got home, we discovered the last revolutionary leader who had helped free Russia from the grip of Communism had been shot on the bridge right behind St. Basil's Cathedral just hours after our departure, and in response, Putin had closed the country from outside visitors. My mind had to wonder, was that pushback from the enemy? Was it that what we went to do had no impact? Then the Lord gently reminded me, I was first called to obedience; second, I was to trust Him. I also needed to realize that what happens on the surface and in politics may be how the world judges the landscape, but that is not how God judges it, and what we see and hear are seldom connected to the spiritual climate. The reality is I may never know in this life, and I am at peace with that. Building my section of the wall and staying focused on it is my assignment, not understanding how it all fits together.

After we completed our assignment but were still in Russia, the Lord took me to the book of Esther. It is a short book, so it was not hard to read through it, but the Lord did not release me from it, I read it several times, praying for discernment as to what God was calling me to. What I heard was He was calling me to another place of spiritual darkness, one in which the story of Esther would prove key, Istanbul, Turkey. Now, at this point, I was downright clueless as to why the Lord would call me there. I had heard about terrorist activities there and bombings, but at that point, that was about all I could recall. I remember thinking, Lord, really, that does not seem like a very safe place to go. Then the familiar, "Do you trust me?" And my familiar, "Yes, Lord, I trust you!"

Chapter Twenty

God's Heart: Istanbul

So, I now knew where my next assignment was but had to wait for when. In the meantime, I started to do some research on this city Istanbul and soon realized its previous names of Byzantium and Constantinople; put more flesh on the bones, as you were. History, lots of history, lots of conquests and battles. Istanbul sits on a narrowing referred to as the Bosphorus, with the Black Sea above and the Sea of Marmara south, which then goes into the Mediterranean Sea. It is the place where Asia meets Europe and the borders of the city are on both continents. It has been a passageway fought over for centuries. The city is a blending of cultures and people, more so than other parts of Turkey might be. As I researched, I discovered so many biblical connections to the part of the world, from where Noah's ark landed, the land of Abraham, the cities of Ephesus, Smyrna, Cappadocia, Tarsus, Pergamon, to name a few. It was part of the Persian Empire, seat of the Ottoman Empire, seat of the Roman and Byzantine empires.

This city was reportedly founded by King Byzas, who wanted to build a great city, and he sought the guidance of the Oracle of Delphi, who told him to build across from the land of the blind. As he travelled and he arrived at the Bosphorus and looked across and said something like, "They must have been blind not to build their city here." Realizing he had referred to the people from this area as blind, he built Byzantium there. As I pondered and prayed about this, I felt that when I got there, I would want to pray about the people there being referred to as blind, as this could be a type of curse, which might make it hard for the people there to see spiritual truth. There was the conquering by the Romans, which had brought Christianity to the area, by the hands of Constantine. It seems being conquered and enslaved does not really make one receptive to the message and may also have contributed to a hardening of hearts to the gospel. Forced religion of any kind is hard to swallow, even if the heart of it was truth, the political baggage gets connected to it. It looked as though there would be lots to pray about as we waited for God's timing.

It has long been a desire to travel on these adventures with my husband, but God has not allowed that to be the case yet, anyway. Eric has been on his own adventures in regards to missions. When God made provision financially for the trip, I was not yet sure who was called to go with me. I asked Eric if he felt called, and we both prayed about it but felt he was not. My oldest son Austin was at a point of transition between jobs, he was willing and able, so it appeared it was God's plan for him to go. I had originally thought early summer, as the price of tickets would be cheaper than within the next month or two, but after talking to Austin about his availability, I threw out the fleece about God confirming the timing by the cost effectiveness of going soon, and to my surprise, it was less expensive than five months out. All the other pieces fell in place too, so we were now planning a trip to Istanbul. The Lord had brought several people across my path that had been to Istanbul and loved it, so that helped alleviate some of my concerns; but there had been a bombing in the area we were heading only a few months prior. God does not give a spirit of fear but of victory, and remember, I trust Him.

My oldest son is very sensitive in lots of ways, spiritually, emotionally, and physically. That is in no way to imply he is weak, he was a powerful football player in high school. He was also the one his peers called at all hours to talk to for guidance or to hear that someone cared about their struggles. I remember the house rule was no phone calls after nine. There would be times I would hear him talking after midnight, and I would go to tell him to get off the phone, only to hear him giving godly counsel to another teenager; rules are not as important as being available when God wants to use you. Austin's journey has been riddled with challenges and roadblocks. But he is one with spiritual insight and gifts, which need to be developed. In speaking to him about the spiritual preparation needed for a trip like this, he, of course, took it seriously. He prayed and then called asking where you find hyssop. Well, that was a good question. I told him I remember it as an herb used for ceremonial cleansing, but I did not remember ever seeing it available anywhere. But we do live in the time of the Internet, and there is very little you cannot find on it, so I did some research and ordered some. Austin, being of the younger generation, had already done the same. There was extra time spent in prayer, fasting, and meditation. You don't want to go into enemy territory carrying baggage which will weigh you down or get used against you or your family.

I did have another dream that I felt was significant two weeks prior to our trip, I found myself in a Jewish temple. I was welcomed in, but as I looked up front and saw the men and the main part of the sanctuary, I was ushered to the left and was seated with a group of elderly Jewish women with head coverings. I sat and listened to the rabbi but could not see him. When I awoke, I had to go back to the book of Esther, maybe it is about "such a time as this," but I felt like I was supposed to go to a Jewish synagogue to a service. The closest Jewish synagogue is an hour away. I went online to see what was available around us and found two listed in Fort Wayne. When I went to the one site, it did not have much information listed, the other spoke of welcoming visitors but to please call ahead to let them know you were coming, as they have some special services not everyone would want to come to. So I called and told them I would like to come, and they told me their services are Friday evening. There being only two Fridays prior to our departure, limited things. I told them I would like to come the coming Friday. She told me we would be welcome but that it was a celebration service, so it would not be their normal service. It was their Purim celebration. So I went home and looked up which celebration it was, knowing it sounded familiar.

Yep, the story of Esther. God's timing is amazing. How He will direct us if we are willing is nothing short of miraculous.

Bless my family, they are good sports, they all agreed to go with me. So my husband and three of my daughters went; Faith was home for a short visit. It was a little uncomfortable going someplace you want to be respectful, but you don't fully understand which customs and traditions have been held onto and which ones have fallen by the wayside over time. My heart was ready to be touched by this beautiful service with traditional music, and the Hebrew language spoken as scripture was read. Well, they did sing in Hebrew, but they put on a play of the Esther story with the theme of South Pacific the movie. It was very different; no connection was made to the lessons and values of Esther. I left very disappointed. The rabbi never spoke to us, never made eye contact; we were invisible. Now, if there had been a large crowd, you would understand, but there were not more than thirty people there including the players, and there were five of us. I left asking God what the purpose of this was. Was it merely a task to test my obedience? Feeling like we had worked through that stage years ago, my heart just felt heavy.

God's chosen people had contemporized things so much they had lost the heart and soul of the story, was that the point? Until I saw it firsthand, I didn't understand how this had to grieve God's heart. May my heart grieve over those things which grieve His. Now, this may not be the situation of all Jewish temples, so I cannot make generalizations from the experience. But I do know better how to pray for that congregation. Heading to a Muslim country, I still did not fully understand the significance of it all. I did feel as though part of the Esther story was about God's big plan being revealed in His perfect way and timing. There is an unfolding you see of connections in the story of relationships which God used between Mordecai and Haman, Esther and the king. God has shown me through this trip and throughout my life how His timing is perfect and complex with layers and layers of connections and threads.

On the day before we left, I felt called to walk and pray around my neighborhood, stopping and praying at each house for the burdens I was aware of. That night, I had a dream. The setting of the dream was my neighborhood, specifically the path I had taken that day to pray. In the dream, I am walking and praying, and I see a bowl, a very ornate white bowl with great detail sitting on the ground in front of me, behind a house in the alley. I look around wondering why this bowl is sitting there and if there are any clues as to whose it is. When I bend down to pick it up, it has a very large misshapen egg; it was a brown egg, not white, with a big bulge on top, which looked like a normal egg except for someone had painted some dots on the top, in a plus sign with a circle of dots around it. Then there were two bulges on the sides just below the top. All of a sudden, the egg cracked, and there were three white birds in it. They were not local birds; they had longer beaks, and the beaks came down on the end a bit and flared out on the top edge a little. I ran my finger along the edge of the bigger baby bird's beak, then I heard another crack, and egg yolk oozed from the bottom of the egg, as if one was undone or not done. I started to head back to my house, and I woke up. This was one of those God dreams. I was awake and present in the dream. I sensed I needed to pay attention to details, and I remembered it all vividly. As I laid in bed, I prayed about it and prayed again for my neighborhood.

    We met Austin in Chicago at the airport. He came from Iowa, which was just about as far a drive we had. We boarded our flight and got settled in for a nonstop flight, which would take just under twelve hours. There was a person sitting between us with a young child. They seemed irritated with the arrangement and asked to be moved to a row with an open seat for the child. Truthfully, I think we were all relieved when a spot was found for them. Shortly after take-off, Austin's physical sensitivity came into play; his body does not like motion, so he threw up for the first three hours of our flight. I was so thankful there was an empty seat between us, it would have been rough for someone to be sitting right next to someone throwing up that long. He finally settled in, and then he slept a while. When he was feeling better, we talked about what we thought God had planned, and he asked if I had a vision or dream, but I told him the only thing was a dream about my neighborhood back home. He asked what I thought the birds were in the dream. I told him my first

IT'S ABOUT HIM

thought was an albatross, then maybe a seagull. As we reached our destination, we noticed lots of seagulls; Austin said he was leaning toward them being seagulls. It was starting to look like the dream the night before may be connected to Istanbul after all.

We got to our hotel, which was in the old town part of Istanbul, across a street from the city wall. Istanbul had a large wall which surrounded the old town and had areas which were in good shape and some in severe decline. It was interesting how many buildings were built into the wall, and the wall was just back from the shoreline. We got our things into our room, and then went out and walked down along the wall and across the street from the shore. As we walked along, we saw evidence of the long history of this place. We arrived at a section in which a palace had been built into the wall, with columns and window frames still seen. This section had some landscaping and bushes. As we were walking by, I saw a downcast man sitting on a ledge behind the bushes with a bottle in a brown sack. I felt called to engage him, so I asked him if he could take a picture. He did not understand any English and gestured so, but then he saw my camera open on my phone, so he took the phone and took a couple of pictures of Austin and I. I smiled and thanked him, and we continued along the wall a bit. Once we turned around and headed back to the hotel, we got to the area where we had met this man who had the appearance of a homeless man. I looked to see if he was still sitting there, and he was; but when he saw us, he lit up and waved. We waved and smiled as we walked by. I told Austin that I felt called to go pray for him. He didn't hesitate to tell me we should head back again. When we came walking back, he jumped up and came over to us, as if he was glad to see us. I put my hand on his shoulder and told him I wanted to pray for him, and since he had not learned English or us Turkish in the short time since our last interaction, I just bowed my head and asked God to bless this man and set him free from the bondage he was under, asking God to reveal Himself to him by the precious name of Jesus. When I lifted my head, the man was weeping, and he thanked me and kissed my hand. Some things don't require translation. As we left him standing, something had changed, I could feel it. Then I looked at Austin and he had tears. I asked him if he was okay, and he said he loved me and as I was praying for the man, he had a vision of a large bat in the sky behind him; and as I prayed, the bat dispersed into thousands of bats and headed toward me. He immediately prayed protection over me, but then realized that the man, who had been standing in darkness, now had radiant light shining down on him and surrounding him, he was free. He restated about the bats and said if the enemy didn't know before, he knew we were there now. My response was he would have figured it out anyway, but the important thing to focus on was that God freed that man! We walked back by the hotel and had dinner there. The hotel had a beautiful terrace which highlighted both the Blue Mosque and Aya Sofia (Hagia Sophia). The restaurant was all glass from the chair rail up, so we had a beautiful view of the Bosphorus to the right and the old city to the left of where I was sitting. Tired from our long trip, we went to our room and had devotions and went to bed.

When I awoke, I heard, "High place." Well, I got up and investigated discovering the high place was on the Asian side and a park called Camlica had been built there and was a popular spot to get away. We would need to figure out the best way to get there, but first we needed to get breakfast and do some exploring.

We had a king's feast for breakfast, with long tables full of food. I have never seen such a display of food in my life, from nuts, fresh fruits, dried fruits, honey and honeycomb, grains, eggs hard boiled, omelets, breakfast meats, several selections of cheeses, breads, and on and on. We ate, and I enjoyed my Turkish tea. Then we went off to explore and get the lay of the land. We needed to get to the square between the Blue Mosque and the Hagia Sophia to get our bus passes for the tour bus we had purchased before arriving. As we walked up the hill to the square, the sight of buildings and square were beautiful. The attention to detail was noted everywhere, and you could feel the depth of time and history as if you could wade through it.

Of course, we screamed tourist, with our dress and skin color, so we had a target on us the whole time. We were approached by a man to show us the beautiful rugs in their family shop, and of course, not wanting to be rude, we found ourselves taken to a second floor display room, and I just kept praying this was legitimate, as I could just see this as a pretense to kidnap someone. They offered us tea, and we politely declined. They insisted, saying they would be offended, it was a part of the culture and that is why they are famous for their Turkish hospitality. So we sat and drank, and they showed us carpets, and they were exquisite, but I did not come for rugs, and even if I wanted one, they were way out of our range. I explained that I appreciated the artistry and time invested, but we could not afford a rug. We thanked them and exited. I would like to say we were smart enough not to get suckered in again, but yet later fell prey to yet another salesman, his tactics were a little different, but we were now onto these guys. They would start out with a line about us not being from there and where did we come from, or they would ask us if we were from Europe or America, then it was how long would we be staying. I would always be vague. Then they would say something about me being Austin's wife, I must assume to flatter me; but after about a dozen times, it just frustrated Austin.

We did find and board our bus, which we could get on and off at our leisure; the routes were set, and another bus would be by in about thirty minutes. Before we boarded, however, we were offered a great deal on a cruise of the Bosphorus, and they stressed what a different perspective the city had from the water. Well, the price was reasonable, and Austin was game. So I went ahead and bought a pass for us to go later in the week. There were so many historical places and so many mosques. They mentioned who built each one as we passed, and the narrative told of how over 99 percent of the residents of Turkey were Muslim, how the number of minarets (towers) was significant in showing the ranking or position of the person who built it. The Blue Mosque had caused quite a stir with six minarets, as it was then in competition with Mecca, so a handsome donation to Mecca cleared up the misunderstanding, and the six minarets were allowed to stay. They spoke of a mosque built to honor a mother of a sultan, and one built on the ground of what had once stood the Church of the Holy Apostles. We went across a bridge to the Asian side and saw a palace called Beylerbeyi (Lord of Lords). My hope was the tour bus would take us up to Camlica, but it did not. It looked like we would have to come up with another way to get there. They spoke of the docks and how the fisherman learned that by grilling their catch on the dock, it saved them having to take their fish to the market, so balik ekmek (fish and bread) is a local favorite. Austin said he wanted to make sure he had some of that before we headed home. I reminded him of our boat ticket, so we should be able to catch one of the fishing boats near the pier when we get back from that excursion. Then we were on the route back to the square in which we started.

The Sultanahmet square was the heart of the old city, with the Milion Stone, near the Basilica Cistern, the Hippodrome, Topkapi Palace, the Archaeological Museum, and of course, either side sits the Blue Mosque and Hagia Sophia. We would save most of these until later in the week as they were all within walking distance of our hotel and our bus pass was only good a couple of days. There was so much here to learn about and to see. It was important to pay attention to details, but we still needed to stay focused on listening to God about what our assignment was.

As I prayed about the dream and its connection to Istanbul, I felt that the egg with three birds represented the three churches which had been converted to mosques, the Chora Church, the Little Hagia Sophia, and the Hagia Sophia. The egg that had not developed into a bird was the one undone, which was where the Fatih Mosque sat on top of the previous Church of the Holy Apostles. It was the only church destroyed and a mosque built in its place. As I reflected on the egg in the bowl, it was one large dome and two small, the detail on the top of the bowl matched the construction of the Hagia Sophia, just below the dome. God is a God of details.

That evening, as I was reading the Bible, the Lord took me to Colossians 3. It was talking about putting off the things of this world and putting on the things of God, like kindness, meekness, humility, forgiveness, and love. Getting away from the routine is always good for seeing things from a different perspective. The next day, we got up early, and I went with Austin for breakfast, but it was a time of fasting for me. I continued to pray about where we were to start.

IT'S ABOUT HIM

After breakfast, we headed to Beylerbeyi Bay on the Asian side, and we would get a taxi to take us up to the high point. We wound our way to the top of the peak in the taxi and were dropped off at the entrance to the park. As we finished the ascent, we dodged many children who had been brought up in large groups. The site was beautiful, landscaped with lots of tulips of all colors arranged in beautiful displays, with some hyacinth to add some color and their beautiful scent. The walkways were inlayed cobblestone, and there were benches, tables and chairs, and a couple of gazebos on top of the peak in which you could overlook the water and the expansive city of fourteen million below. I could just imagine an arrogant king professing from this peak his dominion over all he purveyed, speaking words which could bind a people and create spiritual blindness.

What a great vantage point to pray. We prayed for the light of Christ to shine down and illuminate the hearts and minds of those who reside here, that any blinders to keep them from seeing truth and God's heart for them be removed, and any curse speaking blindness be broken by the power of Jesus Christ and His precious blood. As we prayed over this high point, Austin felt he needed to go and pray at the low point of Istanbul. When we checked, we already had tickets for that vantage point, it was the Sea of Marmara.

We ventured on to see St. Stephen's Church, one of the few churches not converted into a mosque, only to find it covered in scaffolding and under complete renovations due to its condition. We attempted to walk up to the Chora Church from there, but after walking uphill for quite a while and could not find any street signs to help us find our way, we gave up and headed back downhill to get our bearings again. We did end up at the Egyptian Spice Market and were enthralled at the variety of spices, teas, coffee, Turkish delight and just about any other food item or food preparation item you could want. As a lover of teas, I may have gotten a little carried away in the tea shop. It was one of those places which was sensory overload, with bright colors, and an array of smells, people shouting to gain your attention.

We ended up back at the square and saw the Milion Stone, a well-worn obelisk-shaped stone which was the point that the distance to all parts of the Roman Empire was measured from, basically ground zero for the Roman Empire. We prayed that this stone which represented the center of the empire and the starting point for all journeys would not replace the center of Christianity, Christ himself, the cornerstone and the starting point for each of us that accept Christ as our savior.

Nearby was the Hippodrome, which originally sported the chariot races with three obelisks in the middle, one from Egypt of Pharaoh Thutmose III, brought to Istanbul and was broken during transit, so the bottom section is missing, a serpent column in the middle made of bronze which was a spiral of three serpents whose heads were located at the top originally, it came from a temple of Apollo. It was considered evil due to the serpents and was torn apart, with only a remnant at the bottom remaining. The other end had an obelisk which originally was plated with brass depicting the annals of Basil I and has been called the Constantine Obelisk. But over the years, the metal was needed and stripped off, so now it is an unremarkable obelisk with rough stone and holes where the plating had been anchored to the stone.

These were remnants of a time of conquest and games to entertain the elite, which now bring tourists. As we walked and prayed, we prayed that as they once heralded entrance to a tomb, a pagan temple, and of human exploits, power and pride, that they would not hold any spiritual authority or connection to hinder God's work in this place.

The next morning when we awoke, again we reviewed Colossians 3, with emphasis on kindness and humility standing out. We went to breakfast, but it was another morning for me to fast. I prayed about next steps and felt we finally were to go to the Hagia Sophia. When we entered the courtyard, I could imagine Roman processions walking through the main entrance of this beautiful structure.

Now the mosque, once basilica, was the third structure to exist on the site. The first was built by Constantius II in 346–360, but fire destroyed it during a riot. It was rebuilt in 415 and suffered a similar fate in 532. The third attempt was constructed by Justinian in 532–537. He preferred the domed basilica style and had the Little Hagia

Sophia built to make sure it would structurally be sound before the grander Hagia Sophia was built in 527 to 536 AD.

As we entered the church, there was an outer hallway which held relics and was impressive in the detail work in the ceilings and doors. At one end was a video, and as I sat and listened, they mentioned that the Muslim faith holds high regard to the mother-son relationship, which may have been why many of the mosaics and paintings had been spared. Pondering on this, I realized that it was not by accident that this basilica was the key to our journey, and this journey was with my firstborn, a son. We entered and started up a steep cobblestone ramp which turned around and around to get to the upper level. As we walked up, we passed two Muslim mothers trying to maneuver their strollers with their toddlers up this passageway. When we finally reached the top, there were steps to complete the trek. Realizing the struggle these young mothers would have, I waited; and when they neared the top, I reached and picked up the front of the stroller, and Austin did the same for the other mother. We carried them up the steps and set them down.

Then it hit me, one of those you sense it in the spirit; something broke, and I started crying. This was an act of kindness and humility from an American Christian and her son to two Muslim mothers with sons; just a simple gesture, yet it was the living out of Colossians 3. We walked and prayed on the upper level, where there were several mosaics, paintings, and a set of marble doors which represented the door between earth and hell. On the doors and in several places, crosses had been removed, some dug out, so it made a rough groove of the cross; probably not what they intended, but it remained proof of the building's beginning and heritage.

We then went down to the main floor and stood in the center of the dome and prayed for the Lord to break any strongholds, barriers, or curses connected with this once church then mosque and now museum. That the light of Christ would illuminate the darkness and expose it to reveal truth to set the captives free and bring this and all Istanbul and Turkey under the Lordship of Jesus Christ. After praying, I felt I was to walk and pray around the building, but when we got to the back, there was a tall fence and gate which was closed.

Frustrated but figuring God would make a way even if it required getting to the outside wall of the old city.

Next, we took a taxi to Chora Church. It was originally built at the end of the third century, had suffered damage through natural disasters, and was then rebuilt by Justinian in 536. The exterior was covered so it was not visible, tarps on the outside of scaffolding was the only thing visible. We were still able to enter, and there were some of the most beautiful mosaics of Christ and several frescoes adorning the domes and walls.

One of the storylines shown in the mosaics was following that Mary was immaculately conceived and that she was sinless. Although I have utmost respect for Mary, I feel it dishonors Christ and his deity as the Son of God to build up a backstory to make His significance diminish. Mary would not want to be worshiped, I am sure that breaks her heart. We prayed against this and asked for Christ to be glorified.

The next morning, we arose early, again a day of fasting for breakfast; we headed to the Little Hagia Sophia, the third of our white birds. And as we had prepared for the day, it seemed that the focus of Colossians 3 was forgiveness today. My spirit sensed a need to pray with a person of Muslim descent who could pray a prayer of forgiveness with me. Whenever there is unforgiveness, it creates a stronghold or stumbling block in the spiritual realm, those seeds take root and can consume lives and cultures. When Rome conquered Byzantium, it enslaved people; it forced Christianity on the people, and Christianity took on a political facet as we have mentioned before. There has also been harm brought against Christians by the Muslims, which is why a reciprocating prayer can be so powerful, it breaks things on both sides. I can ask God to forgive us of the sins committed against these people, but it does not hold the same weight as if someone that represents that group of victims can pray in agreement and accept my repentance and sorrow for what transpired against them. That is why where two or more are gathered in Christ's name, He is there.

Well, there were a couple of issues with this situation. One, I knew no Muslims here; of the over 99 percent of fourteen million people who are Muslim in this city, I did not know any on a first-name basis that I could make this kind of request of, not something you usually approach a stranger with. Not only did they need to be Muslim, they needed to understand English well enough to understand what I was asking. Then they had to be willing to pray with an American Christian about forgiveness in the name of Jesus Christ. Well, it was absolutely plain to me that God would need to do the miraculous to bring this to pass; but you know me by now, I believe in a God of miracles.

We got to the mosque early, and it had not yet opened. There was a man sitting on a bench, I suspected he was one who tried to earn money giving tours. As we stood and waited for it to open, he approached us. He spoke English very well. He was born in Turkey and lived a while in Germany and then returned to Turkey and Istanbul about twenty-eight years previous. He started sharing his frustration at the state of the world, where people have to live in fear because of terrorists. He commented, even though he and others are Muslim, their lives do not matter to these extremists. I smiled and told him that there can never be true peace except under the Lordship of Jesus Christ, that is the heart of the problem. It came as a shock as he uttered the words, "Oh, how I love Jesus," and his eyes swelled with tears. He proceeded to tell me that a young pastor had come through several years before and shared Christ with him. He has prayed to Christ ever since.

He did ask if he could share some of the history of this church/mosque, even though I sensed some bristling in Austin. We went into the building, and he shared about the past of this beautiful building. Austin stepped away, bless his heart; he was the shield protecting us as we spoke. He had a severe headache and some dizziness come upon him, which he knew was a spiritual attack. After he showed us the interior, we were standing on a balcony under the main dome. I asked him for a favor, and his initial response was "anything." I cautioned him this was not the kind of request he should agree to without understanding what I was asking him. I explained that God had brought me to Istanbul to pray for the people here to come under the Lordship of Jesus Christ and to ask for forgiveness as a Christian for any harm that has been done under the guise of Christianity toward the Muslims, and as an American toward the Turkish, and I asked him to reciprocate that any harm done by Muslims against Christians or Turkish against Americans would be repented of so we could break those spiritual strongholds.

He looked me in the eye and said, "Yes, I will pray with you in agreement for these things." So we stood in this building, which has been a place of worship for Christians from the sixth century to a place of worship for Muslims, and prayed for forgiveness and healing in the name of Jesus Christ. Once we finished, we all had tears running down our cheeks, and he informed me that he would never forget this, that this was the most special and sacred thing.

We left the building, and I stood for a second in awe of the living God who could pull this off, because of His love for these people who are lost in darkness. Later, as I was deleting random pictures of the ground or some other thing I didn't intend to take a picture of, I found two photos which I did not remember taking. They were not a good photo of the building; it was just of the edge of the building right next to the entrance, but as I looked closer, I realized that there was a beam of light shining down where the door was at, and on the edge of the beam of light is a rainbow. It was in both like confirmation that it was not a fluke. There was blue sky, no clouds. I have no idea where that beam of light came from. No, I take that back, I do know, but the fact that God would go to the trouble is amazing. God is a God of details. He cares about the details. And if we take the time, we will see Him reveal Himself in details all around us. We walked away from there stunned by God's love, mercy, and provision. It was a day about forgiveness.

We then walked to the square and, around the corner, went into the Basilica Cistern. There was built a huge underground cistern to hold water for the palace. Hundreds of columns were brought in to support it from Roman buildings all around the empire. There is one column with eyes all over it which appear to be crying due to the moisture, and it is in memory of the hundreds of lives lost building the cistern. As with so many things in history, it is hard to fathom what things cost, but there is a cost for everything, sin is the big one, and Christ was willing to pay the cost, the debt, even though He was the only one in history who could have claimed complete innocence, but He chose to pay the debt knowing we could not. Thank you, Jesus.

We then found a taxi and went to Fatih Mosque, which is the only site we went to that the original church was completely destroyed. The Church of the Holy Apostles had held several relics from the apostles and held the tombs of Roman emperors. It had been damaged by earthquakes and ransacked. When Fatih the Conqueror reclaimed Istanbul for Turkey, he cleared the site and built a mosque on the land on the hillside. We walked and prayed. I also had to pray forgiveness toward our taxi driver who charged us ninety-four lira for a ride that should have cost fourteen. He insisted that was what was owed, so I paid it. He said the trip back would be much less; of course, that was because he would not be sticking around to take us. Immediately, I chose to forgive him, as I knew it had to be out of desperation that he had cheated us. Obviously, the lesson that day about forgiveness was not yet over. I must confess, I have gone back and recommitted to the decision to forgive him, as I feel the frustration build even now thinking about it. Forgiveness is the right path; it is not the easy one.

We did have the opportunity to meet a young man who was from our community in Indiana, who had come to participate in the culture of Istanbul for college. It is such a small world. During our conversation with him, he had discovered the Turkish were very superstitious and do not typically take their children out into the public until they are older, because if someone looked at them with "the evil eye," they would be cursed. In their culture, to look at someone with a glance of anger, annoyance, or frustration put a curse on them. So I asked what was up with all the single eyes, usually in blue, that I saw all over, in windows, taxis, shops. They are like a talisman to ward off the evil eye. Interesting for a culture which started on the premise that these people were blind that an eye would become a symbol of hope and protection. Praying that they would not trust in superstitions but in the living God who sees all and knows all.

We then met up for our boat tour. We expected the bus to take us down to the pier where all the fishing boats were docked and several touring boats. We were surprised that we ended up walking down behind and past our hotel, which was about a mile away from the square, to this lone pier along the shore. We stood and waited, and eventually, our tour boat docked, and we looked up and down this vacant section of beach, and there were no other piers or boats to be seen along this section. Austin was disappointed as this was supposed to be near the fishing boats so he could get his balik ekmek. He said "no fish and bread" for him.

As we were out on the boat and went onto the Sea of Marmara, Austin and I prayed. I prayed that God would bless these people, that the Living Water of Christ would cleanse them and nourish their souls. I also prayed that God would bring in the harvest, raise up fishers of men in this country. As we finished our cruise, we did see the city from a different perspective. When we came back to our pier, that lonely pier we docked, I was shocked to see a man on the beach at the end of the pier selling balik ekmek. We just laughed, but then the picture of Christ on the shore cooking fish for the disciples as they came in off the boat was there, and I realized that rekindling of the calling on Austin's life to be a fisher of men. As I looked at him, I simply asked if he "got it." With a serious response, he said yes, he got it. Matthew 4 talks about the high places that satan took Jesus, promising power over all the kingdoms of the world, and Christ understood worldly power offered nothing eternal. Then in the same chapter, he begins calling his disciples, and when he comes upon them, there they were casting their nets into the sea, and Jesus called them to be fishers of men.

What a day it had been! We were down to one day left in Istanbul. As we debriefed at the end of the day and I was doing my devotions, I told Austin that even though we had been to the three churches/mosques which were representative of the three white birds and the mosque on the grounds of the one undone, I did not yet have a sense we were done yet. We sat and prayed. Austin then spoke up, "Momma, you know how you first thought the white birds were albatross? Well, I think you were right. I just looked it up and they represent a burden or curse." Then he sat a minute and asked what the significance of the minarets were, and I checked, they are a lighthouse, a watchtower, they are where the call to prayer is given from; they also represent a gate between earth and heaven. He asked if any of the mosques had three minarets, and I told him none that I could remember. I was relatively certain the Hagia Sophia had four. So I looked at the picture I had taken, and what did I see! Three white minarets, and one red brick one that looked like it had not been finished. Sound familiar? Three white and one undone. Just to top it off, the red minaret was the last one built, by guess who, Fatih the Conqueror. Have I mentioned God is a God of details?

The next morning, we got up and went directly to the Hagia Sophia to pray about the minarets and what they represented. I still had not walked around the Hagia Sophia and I sensed I needed to do that. The only minaret which I could reach to touch was the red one. Austin suggested that when we had headed back that way on our walk to the boat, that there may have been a narrow walkway we could fit in behind the building. So we headed there, and sure enough, there was. So we walked and prayed three laps and then part of a fourth (you know, one undone), stopped to lay hands on the red minaret and pray God's blessing and redemption of what these stand for with the three white to no longer be represented by albatross but rather doves of peace and purity, and the one undone, being the red one, representing the precious blood of Christ, which has the power to wash away the sins and redeem. We also prayed that God would put His watchmen on the towers to protect and proclaim the good news of Jesus.

Then it was finished, our assignment had been completed. And I heard it's "a new day dawning" in my head as the sun was on the rise. God is good. He is great. He is amazing. He is worthy of our praise. And He is in the details.

One of the interesting things is how satan deceives people, how he allows truth to be a part of some religions, but a subtle or sometimes a not so subtle twist changes it from truth to a lie. Prior to Mohammed, the Arabs were independent tribes and bands of nomads who had no common ground; he brought them together

Chapter Twenty-One

An Unexpected Find Old Quebec City

Being back only a few months from my last prayer assignment, I was surprised when I heard the call for another one. Not only was this soon for another trip, it just seemed different, probably because it was on our continent. It was my fourteen-year-old daughter we felt was to go. So trying to work the trip in before returning to school and after a very busy summer gave a tight timeframe to pull this trip off. After investigating costs for flights, we decided renting a car made most sense. This journey was taking me north into Canada, specifically Quebec. One day, mid-July, I was in prayer thanking God for the opportunities He has blessed me with when I began listing the places He has taken me, Quebec jumped in the listing. I hesitated and prayed about it and felt I was to go to Quebec's Old City. The strange thing is, Quebec is another place I have never thought about travelling to, and I did not even know if Quebec's Old City existed. Once I got done praying, I went to the computer to see if such a place existed. Of course, it did! You would think by now He wouldn't shock me, but yet again, He did. Not only did it exist, but the history was so much more significant than expected. It is the only remaining walled city in North America, it is home to the oldest stone church in North America, it has one of the seven Holy Doors in the world, and the only one outside of Europe, and it is a sister city to Istanbul. It is French in culture and language.

There was not the normal preparation time for this trip, so as I prayed about the journey, the Lord kept bringing me to the angel Gabriel. I studied every scripture he was mentioned in in the Bible. He was there with Daniel, Mary, Elizabeth, and Zechariah. Gabriel was a messenger for God. He helped Daniel understand the visions, he told these individuals that they were highly favored and esteemed. He gave messages directly from God to these people. What a blessing to hear actual words, that way they did not get in the way of the message trying to discern what they heard in their spirit. It had to be both frightening and encouraging. It would make you more determined and help your faith grow. As I continued to look into the angel Gabriel, I discovered that he is found in the Muslim faith also. Mohammed reported being visited by the angel Gabriel. One thing I do realize was that there are people who have gotten off track and began worshipping angels rather than the one who created them. I would wait to see if Gabriel had anything to do with this journey.

On to the next adventure, I was looking forward to the long drive with Grace. She is the quiet one of my kids, she does not like to talk, she hates answering questions, and she is fourteen. My hope was that the silence would wear her down and she would talk and share what she is thinking about, about the relationships in her life . . . yes, I was outside my mind. The one thing that did light her up was the possibility of a road trip when she was a senior with her friends, and she asked a lot of questions about what they could do, where they could go. The adventure bug has gotten her, although it is way cooler to go with friends than your mom. I get it.

We took two days to drive there, ten or so hours of the sixteen-to-seventeen-hour drive the first day. On the second day, we could not get into our accommodations until after four o'clock, so we stopped over in Montreal for a quick visit of the Notre Dame Basilica. The pictures I had seen were breathtaking. It truly was a magnificent structure. The question I had to ask was, do we do this for God's glory or ours? This particular cathedral was one the architect was so pleased with. He converted to Catholicism on his death-bed so he could be buried there. If what we offer is our best to bring God glory, that is good, but I wonder if our motives are ever that pure. I love the craftsmanship and beauty of the majestic cathedrals. But when I see the money still being poured into them to maintain them, and knowing the money and sacrifice that went into the design and construction to begin with, my mind has to wonder if when Christ rose from the grave and God no longer resided in a temple or ark of the covenant and we became the temple, maybe, instead of building big megachurches, we should be building up and investing in people. We are seeing more churches investing in building their churches around the ministries God has called them into or leasing space in existing buildings which aren't open on Sunday, I think that there is wisdom in checking our hearts and motives and trying to use the resources God has given us to make the greatest impact on lives. Why is it so hard not to get caught up in investing in things rather than people? What we get to take to heaven will not be our houses, cars, jewelry, our fancy churches, or our collections but the people we have helped find Christ, they will be there for eternity. Such a better investment, isn't it?

As we walked outside of this beautiful building, I found it interesting that there were a row of shops selling Hindu idols and pagan items right across the street. Darkness is ever pushing in, gaining ground if we are not diligent.

We found our way back to our vehicle and finished our journey to the bed-and-breakfast we would be staying at. We were greeted by a sweet woman named Patricia, who led us to our rooms. We had one small room with a twin bed and then in the attic was a lovely room with a big bed, several comfortable chairs, and a desk. My asthma did not like the steep ascent into the attic, and there was no air-conditioning in the building, so I deferred Grace to the attic room, which was way cool with her. I could not imagine trying to carefully and quietly get up and down that stairway to get to a bathroom in the middle of the night. The arrangement did not lend itself to the bonding I had hoped for; but I know God, He can and will use it for His purposes.

We found Quebec's Old City charming; it is a city on a hill, with the narrow cobblestone streets and a European feel in the architecture and even in the air. There was a general store just down the hill from our B and B. It was a great find; they had fresh fruits and vegetables, some readymade dishes, some desserts, a deli, a room of spices, and all kinds of epicurean delights from syrups, jams, teas, maple everything, and cold beverages. There were many charming shops, but I had to remind myself that is not what we came for. We walked around the neighborhood and prayed. We did buy some cold sparkling water and a soda for Grace and headed back to the inn to get settled in for the night.

The Lord had not yet really defined our purpose and plan, and there had been no vision or dream. I prayed and read the scriptures, but nothing was really speaking to me, so I went to sleep. I was awoken in the middle of the night with a disturbing dream. I was with a group of people and we were at a doorway with a stairway down. There was a lady in front of me, she turned to face me, like she was going to speak to this group I was with, when someone from behind me reached over my shoulder and pushed the lady down the stairs. I stood in horror as I watched this lady fall down the steps. I ran down to check on her, and people were trying to help her get up. I went into medical mode and was telling people not to touch her, she could have broken her neck or back. And as I was watching this reflexive twitching in her legs, I was sure something was seriously wrong. It was so frustrating. I was trying get someone to go get help for her as I tried to calm her and keep her still, and no one was listening to anything. I decided if I didn't go get help, no one would, so I stood and started looking for help, then I woke up. Those kind of disturbing dreams, I do not like. I prayed a bit and fell back to sleep.

At daylight, we went down to breakfast, and there was an older couple there already, and they were conversing with each other in French, as we came in and sat down. It didn't take long for them to realize we didn't speak or understand French. Our hostess came in, and she chatted with them in French and then with us in English. The couple knew a little English, definitely more English than we did French, and they asked our plans for the day. We told them we

so you could see where the door and sides of the foundation stones were under glass, exposed so you could see.

After everyone else had left, the young man shared how Champlain's wife was twenty-two when she had wed him at forty-four, and he had married her for her dowry to help fund his expeditions, not out of love. She returned to France after being there four years to become a nun. So I took some time to pray that the foundation of this church rest squarely on Jesus Christ and the foundation of greed and arrogance be broken to open hearts to the saving grace of Jesus Christ, to experience purpose beyond material and financial gain, rather spiritual, mental and emotional gain, experiencing the fruits of the Spirit, investing in lives and souls.

When we got back to the top of the hill and the wall, the statue in the circle of Dufferin Terrace was of Champlain with the angel Gabriel with his horn underneath. I also prayed here that the things of heaven not be put below the things of man. As we walked back toward our lodgings, we walked a large section of the wall, praying for God's wall of protection and a tearing down of walls and barriers to the gospel.

Once we walked as far as we could, we had covered three of the four original gateways into the upper city. Gateways always suggest gatekeepers, and in the spiritual, there can be spiritual gatekeepers, so we ask that all gatekeepers be placed and anointed by Jesus Himself, that evil would no longer be in control.

When we got close to the B&B, we stopped in the shop and got cold beverages and some fresh fruit.

I purchased extra, feeling we would run into someone who needed it.

The next day, we headed to the Notre Dame de Quebec, the oldest stone church in North America and the home of the only Holy Door outside of Europe. It was a beautiful structure with ornate gold details above the altar. We did go through the Holy Door and placed in the basket of petitions and prayers. My prayer for this nation was that there would be an outpouring of the Holy Spirit to transform and change lives for the Kingdom and that all things would come under the Lordship of Jesus Christ for God's glory.

When we left there, we walked more of the wall and ended back on the road to which was our main reference point since it was just a block off of our inn. The bag with water and fruit was still in my hand being carried; I had been carrying it several hours by now, and we came up a T street into our road. We crossed over to the side we would need to get either the car or to our B&B. As soon as I got across, I saw him, a man obscured by the street light posts and signs, right on the corner; he was opposite of the corner we had just crossed over, in a wheelchair. I went to cross back over, and poor Grace thought I had lost my mind, reminding me we had just gotten across the road, why was I crossing back, as I held up the bag and gestured toward the man. As soon as she saw him, she understood. So I crossed over and handed the man the bag. He happened to speak English well, so when I told him that this was just a small token but that my prayer is the God would bless him and protect him, he smiled and said, "God bless you." I assured him I was very blessed and wanted to pass it on. He reached for his necklace and said he was blessed too. Then he took my hand and kissed it.

As I turned and left him, it was a flashback of Istanbul where another homeless man kissed my left hand also. I stood and wept. There is something very powerful about receiving a blessing from someone who has nothing. Somehow, these men were connected in the spiritual, and I again stood humbled that God would allow me to be blessed in such a precious way.

When we left there, we went and got the car and headed to St. Anne Canyon and falls. This was another special place as we saw the calm water above the fall; a simple spring that joined other springs and brooks together to create this beautiful waterfall and canyon. Such power when unleashed. I had been praying for an outpouring of the Holy Spirit in our nation, but the vision I see is water churning and building momentum but held back, but oh, the power that will be unleashed when God pulls back His hand. It is a matter of His perfect timing. My prayer as we walked along and across this canyon was that God would allow the movement of the Holy Spirit to bring the power and authority of Christ as a display to break through those things hindering a revival and movement of God in this continent, an unleashing of His Living Water.

The next day, we were heading out for the two-day drive home. As I awoke, I had a voice in my head spouting a litany of profanity, and it told me to take my —— Bible and get out of here. Immediately, I recognized it as a spirit of profanity. It required some sincere prayer to break its hold, and my prayer was to bind it and cast it out to not affect anyone else. Well, my solace was that I made the enemy angry, so I accomplished something. The work here was done. We had the opportunity to put some things in the right order, to pray for people, to bless some, to pray over strongholds, walls, and barriers to the gospel, to walk and claim this quaint part of Quebec City for the Lord Jesus. You know how I have mentioned God's timing, this visit fell during their annual "Defile" or parade remembering their history and traditions. How interesting the French word for parade is "defile," and that God would send us to reclaim Quebec's Old City unto Himself in the middle of this celebration. There are no accidents when you live a life surrendered to Christ; God is always in the details.

Chapter Twenty-Two

Belize and the Mayan

A friend approached me and asked if I would go with her to Belize. This is an annual trek for her, although often she takes a sizable team with her. It has been a great avenue to get people's feet wet in a foreign country, with reasonable expense and distance. It also serves as her way of blessing and investing in missionaries from our church who serve there. This trip was starting differently. She had one friend going, and I was the second person she felt she was to ask. Since this call came differently, I felt I had to pray about it. Once I did, the Lord gave me a dream in which was specific to the Mayan people and in a medical setting. It seemed like confirmation to me, so I told her I would go, but that I had a prayer assignment.

Now she is an amazing servant, a hands-and-feet, get-in-and-work kind of servant. If she sees something needing done, she makes sure it gets done. She absolutely believes in prayer and has been investing in the lives of youths, teaching them, and discipling them her entire adult life. She, however, is not quite sure what to think of me. So when she heard prayer assignment, she suggested I touch base with our missionaries.

Our missionaries are friends of mine who I love and I know love me. So when I emailed them about coming to pray, their delay in responding made me a little nervous. Usually, I hear back from them quickly. It was several days, and the tone of the email was hesitant, saying they weren't sure they had the bandwidth to fit a prayer assignment into the schedule as they would be our transportation and have a very busy and active schedule with responsibilities. They were happy to have me come visit and hang out with them.

When I spoke with the friend who invited me to go with her, she said they were concerned about me stirring things up by coming. Well, I was not expecting that response. So I did what I do: I went to the Lord in prayer and told Him that if they did not want me to go to pray, I would not go. At this point in my life, I have to expend my energy strategically. Well, the Lord came right back and put me in line. He asked, "Are you going to please them or to please me?" Well, since He put it that way . . . I emailed my friends in Belize and told them I would be coming and that they did not have to do anything, God would put me where I needed to be and take care of all the details. They did not have to be concerned about altering plans.

Yes, this was an awkward and slightly stressful situation for all of us. We were all going to be stretched in one way or another or possibly in many ways. That is how it goes sometimes. If it was all smooth and easy, it would not be so adventure-like. Dealing with darkness can be intimidating, I get that, but light dispels darkness. We have light; actually we have the Light, and God does not give us a spirit of fear.

I had mentioned the dream the Lord gave me when I prayed about whether I was to go or not. Well, the dream was very specific. I was standing in a room where a doctor was working on a patient. He called me over and asked if I had any ideas to help this patient as there were such limited resources. I walked over to him and looked at the patient's leg, then saw behind him a row of children, cookie-cutter children, who all looked the same; the interesting thing was that they all had matching tattoos on their faces, but the tattoos where under their skin, not on top of it. They just stood and watched us. The doctor asked me to look for something, and I went to a cabinet door and opened it; the children seemed afraid. There was nothing there, so I went to the side where there was a bigger door, and when I opened it, a very deep dark voice said something, something I could not understand, but that made the children recoil in fear. As soon as I heard the voice, I gently closed the door and stated that something big and dark was in there. Then I woke up. Upon awakening, I asked the Lord for clarification of what this dream represented. First was the fact that the Mayan culture was more than skin deep, it was below the surface of what you see, and it had continued to impact and be passed from generation to generation (a generational curse and stronghold). The other thing was a spirit of fear has a stronghold and is influencing and affecting the nation. This helped give me a strategy to pray for this people group even before I arrived in Belize. Knowing that this spirit of fear was affecting the nation, I wondered if the oppression was also affecting my friends, who are there trying to be a living example of Christ and to disciple the people of Belize.

The other lady going was someone my age I had met from another area school that I had not connected with for many years; I was excited for the opportunity to reconnect with her too. The trip down was uneventful, and it was good to see our friends in Belize. They have recently gone from an education-focused mission organization bringing teams down to help improve awareness and gain sponsorships for students who would have to stop their education at equivalent to eighth grade to one focusing on medical missions.

On our first morning in Belize, we went to the compound of their new organization, where we met a team from southern United States. This was to be their last day of clinics in a nearby village. We were asked if we would be willing to help out. The head of the team was told I was a physical therapist and that they may be able to use me too. Someone in the team quickly said that everyone on the team had to have a review of their credentials before they were allowed to work on the team. We told them we were willing to do whatever would be helpful. The wife of the couple in charge of the complex came up to me and said she had heard I was a PT, and I confirmed that I was. She said that was great, because the only medical discipline which does not require credentialing is PT, so they would like to use me, if I did not mind. Of course, it would be the exception to the rule; God had already made a way.

Once we got to the building we were to see patients at, one of our trio was asked to educate about healthy eating and one was to

It was my hope that helped explained why I had to be obedient and come. Knowing God loves them and wants good things for them and their ministry, breaking strongholds and generational curses would bring new freedom for the Mayans to grow deeper in their faith, and it was my prayer that it would make their work more fruitful. They seemed more at peace.

We were then blessed to worship with them in their church and witness several baptisms. That was a day to spend worshiping and sharing, a very low-key kind of day. The Lord did give me scriptures for the next day: Romans 12:1 and 1 Peter 2:5.

The next day, we were headed to the Mayan ruins. At breakfast, I felt I needed to take a piece of fry jack (fried flat bread) for later. On the way there, I asked to stop and get drinks. Fortunately, the shop we stopped at had grape juice, and I knew I was prepared then.

For this adventure, the husband accompanied the three of us, and we met up with our guide. They had booked their usual guide, Deno. When I asked if he was a Christian, they were not sure. As we walked and heard of the stories and history here, I found it amazing that they are still currently excavating new sites in the ruins we were walking through. Knowing that these people lived here eight hundred years after Christ was here and yet they had not yet heard of him. They were a brutal culture where human sacrifice was common. They were very spiritually driven, trying to win favor and appease the several gods they served.

As we walked, I prayed. My mind kept wondering how the sins of the forefathers were affecting the people now. Deno told us he was 80 percent Mayan and grew up playing and climbing these ruins, before security really existed for the site. We eventually made it to the top of the big temple (130 feet), which, not loving heights myself, was in its own right an accomplishment. My friend who had invited me did not make the climb due to arthritic knees, so with the guide, there were just four of us going up together. When I got to the front at the top, the limestone ledge did not seem very wide, so I leaned against the wall while people were walking in front of me, some sitting on the edge. It sure made me nervous for them. I then stood with my friend and read Romans 12:1. "Therefore, I urge you, brothers and sisters, in view of God's mercy, to offer your bodies as living sacrifice, holy and pleasing to God—this is your true and proper worship." Then I read 1 Peter 2:5. "You also, like living stones, are being built into a spiritual house to be a holy priesthood, offering spiritual sacrifices acceptable to God through Jesus Christ." How amazing to stand where priests had once made human sacrifices to appease their gods and claim that Jesus Christ is Lord above all and that He is calling us all to be living sacrifices, that is choosing to live lives blessing and serving others for God's glory.

When we looked down to the lower level of the temple, there was a small building, which Deno told us is where they prepared the sacrifices. Deno was ahead of us and headed down to the level where our friend was waiting, so the three of us stopped and had communion, remembering the greatest of all sacrifices, the one which completed the work that God had called Christ to.

After going down to the ground level, we continued our tour. At one point, I was left with Deno as our missionary friend was fishing for tarantulas. It seemed like the time to speak with him, so I asked him how he balanced his cultural heritage and religion with what we know today. He said no one had ever asked him that. He was not sure he had ever really thought about it from that perspective. So I asked him whom he worshiped. He said "God." I asked him which god since we had discussed so many. His response was "the creator God." Then I asked him where Christ fit for him. He said, "He is my Savior." He shared how he had come to faith in Christ.

It was then that I shared how God will send me to pray for spiritual breakthrough and to break strongholds. I shared my dream about the Mayan children and how the culture is more than skin deep, it is under the surface and it has been handed down from generation to generation, creating strongholds and generational curses passed through the bloodline. He said that was absolutely right. When I asked if he would pray in agreement to break these to allow a deeper relationship and understanding of God's heart for the Mayan people and to deepen their walk with Jesus Christ, he wholeheartedly agreed. So we stood in the Mayan ruins and prayed, claiming victory in the precious name of Jesus over these generational curses, strong-

"Yes, Lord, I trust you with all I have and all I am, I am yours."

What will your answer be when he asks you? Trust Him, His ways are so much better than the world's. He is calling you to surrender, to trust, to follow. How do I know this? Because He has allowed me to see His heart for the least of these, and it will take all of us working together to bring His Kingdom on Earth as it is in heaven. He is calling you, don't turn away from living your life fully alive. Don't settle for the hollow shadow life that satan wants us to settle for.

This is not the end of my story; I wait expectantly for where the Lord will call me next. In the meantime, I choose to serve Him where I am now. May I be used to bless others and in turn bless Him. I have to know Him, I have to serve Him, it is the call. Remember, it is not only my call, it is your call too. May the Lord Jesus bless you on your journey and your adventures.

About the Author

In a book titled *It's About Him*, it seems counterintuitive to write much about the author. The author is of no real consequence; she lives in a small rural community in north central Indiana, with a family, including her loving and supportive husband of nearly thirty-four years and the two youngest of their six children. She is an ordinary woman, committed to the amazing savior, Jesus Christ. She desires to be a blessing and to minister each day in a broken and needy world. She serves as a physical therapist, as a wife, mother, friend, and as an intercessor. What she hopes and prays is that interwoven in her story, you will see the living God who is not only real, but is calling people to make themselves available to be used; ordinary people, people like her.